FRIDAY HARBOR &

SAN JUAN ISLAND

Umbrella Guide to:

FRIDAY HARBOR &

SAN JUAN ISLAND

by

JEROME K. MILLER

UMBRELLA
BOOKS

Published and distributed by:

UMBRELLA BOOKS

a division of Harbor View Publications Group

440 Tucker Ave., P.O. Box 1460

Friday Harbor, WA 98250-1460

Cover photo: A Washington state ferry approaching
Friday Harbor. Historic Spring St. is above the ferry.

Frontispiece: A Columbia Black-tail Deer in the spring,
when his new antlers were in the "fuzz" stage.

DEDICATION

for

MARILYN DAYTON

a splendid coworker

TABLE OF CONTENTS

INTRODUCTION

This little book was designed for visitors to Friday Harbor and San Juan Island, in Washington State. Compiling the information for this book would not have been possible without the assistance and encouragement of many people including: Peggy Anderson, Lee Bave, Nate Benedict, C.O. Brown, Inez Browne, Linda Browne, Gordon Buchanan, Hugh and Micky Cahail, Jim Capron, Alan Carter, Neil Carter, Marie Collins, Cliff Dightman, Kenny Dougherty, Marguerite Duyff, Eric Erickson, E.A. (Bud) Geneste, Jess Groll, Herb and Martha Gubelman, Dick Hoffman, Garreth Jeffers, Blair King, Lorane Larson, Roger Loring, Edith Martel, Ethel Martin, Bill Mason, Ross Miner, Al and Priscilla Nash, Charlie Nash, Wendy F. Picinich, Jessica Porter, Tim Ransom, Juanita Rouleau, Frances Seels, Clyde Sundstrom, Fred and Nadine Sundstrom, Dion B.C. Sutton, Neil Tarte, and Ed Wilke.

Several published sources have been particularly valuable. The most important being *San Juan: The Powder-Keg Island* by Jo Bailey-Cummings and Al Cummings. Other useful publications were *Friday Harbor Then and Now*, by F.H. VanCleve, *Pig War Islands*, by David Richardson, *Birds of the San Juan Islands,* by Mark Lewis and Fred Sharp, a 1901 *Illustrated Supplement to The San Juan Islander, and Who the Hell Was San Juan?* by Doug Cardle, plus many issues of the *San Juan Islands Almanac* and the *Journal of the San Juans.* Don Hood, the president of the San Juan Horticultural Society granted permission to reproduce the society's guide to the Jakle's Lagoon nature trail.

Special thanks is due to Etta Egeland, the island's preeminent historian and the guiding light for the San Juan Island Historical Society Museum. She graciously provided a wealth of information and encouragement as this book progressed.

Thanks also to Jo Bailey-Cummings for reading the manuscript and spotting many errors. Technical support was provided by Island Technologies and Harbor Press. The photographs were supplied by John Dustrude. The maps were supplied by King Typesetting.

This book is certain to contain errors, which are solely the author's fault. Readers are encouraged to call the author's attention to errors and omissions, so they can be corrected in future editions.

EMERGENCY PHONE NUMBERS:

SHERIFF, FIRE, AMBULANCE 911

Non-emergency calls ....(206) 378-4151

Inter-Island Medical Center ....(206) 378-2141

Evening and weekend emergencies 911

Forest Fire Reports ....(800) 562-6010

FBI ....(206) 622-0460

Poison Information Center ....(206) 442-5495

INFORMATION NUMBERS:

San Juan Island Tourist Information ....(206) 378-2240

Canadian Customs (Victoria) ....(604) 388-3339

US Customs Service (Friday Harbor) ....(206) 378-2080

US National Park Service .....(206) 378-2240 or (206) 378-4184

Washington State Ferries .....(800) 542-0810 or (800) 542-7052

Washington State Tourist Information ....(800) 652-4570

CHAPTER ONE:

ISLAND PEOPLE

The island has a year-round population of a little over 4,000 people. Some are rich and some are poor, but most are middle class. Most are newcomers, but a few have deep island roots. The population includes a few overachievers and some incurably lazy folks, but most are energetic--yet slightly laid back. Categorizing such a diverse population is risky, but the following categories come to mind:

Old Island Families: A few residents trace their roots to early island settlers. Names like Bailer, Boyce, Firth, Fleming, Guard, Hannah, Larson, Lawson, Sandwith, Sundstrom Sweeny, and Wotton, appear in nineteenth century census records and some of their descendants are here today. Those who went to college usually found employment elsewhere, so those who remained usually had a high school education. They work in many fields, including logging, fishing, farming, and the building trades. Others work for government agencies and the utility companies. Many who left the island in their youth have returned for retirement.

Retirees: Thousands of island residents visited the islands during their working years, then moved here when they retired. They came from all parts of the world, but most came from California, Washington, and Alaska. The retirees pursued a variety of demanding careers. Many were doctors, dentists, lawyers, engineers, professors, accountants, military officers, journalists, advertising executives, business owners, and corporate executives. Their diverse skills are a valuable asset to the community.

Business Owners: Most business owners are new residents. They frequently held important positions in other communities and now use their skills in the small but competitive island business community. A few business owners are members of old island families and they may be some of the most influential people in the community.

Self-Employed Professionals: Many residents moved here in mid- career to pursue their professions in the comfort and beauty of the island. They include authors, artists, dentists, consultants, engineers, publishers, and many more. Most accept a reduced income in exchange for living on the island. As a group, they tend to be extraordinarily vigilant about promoting good schools and protecting their physical and social environment.

Government Employees: Over one third of the employed residents work for tax-supported agencies. Major employers are the school district, the county, the town, the port district, the Post Office, the Washington State Ferries, the National Park Service, and the Customs Service. Government jobs are popular as the salaries and benefits are superior to those offered in the private sector.

Private Sector Employees: Major employment groups include fishing, logging, banking, utilities, transportation, tourist services, medical services, building trades, and retail operations. Workers in fishing, logging, and tourist services are frequently unemployed in the winter.

Commuters: The time, expense, and inconvenience of commuting discourages most mainland workers from living on the island. However, the beauty of the island proves irresistible to some, especially to fliers. Several airline captains stationed at Seattle-Tacoma International Airport live on the island. An airline pilot stationed in Minneapolis lives here during his time off. Two financial consultants commute by private plane to the mainland. One works in Seattle and the other works in Mount Vernon. An engineer and an attorney commute to San Francisco.

Hippies: During the 1960's, the island became a home for a large number of young dropouts from mainstream society. They were commonly called "Hippies," though other names may have been more appropriate. Many eventually left the island, but a few remained. Today, they may cut their hair a little shorter and dress more conventionally, but their goal of peace, freedom, and dignity frequently remains uncompromised. The Hippies who were once scorned are usually accepted today as good friends and neighbors.

The Super Rich: The island provides a year-round or summer home to a few very wealthy individuals. Most live in beautiful homes, but avoid displaying their wealth. Several are generous in supporting local nonprofit services. One wealthy couple have become beloved financial angels to local art organizations. Their donations are usually made anonymously, but their identity is well known.

Those who display conspicuous wealth are usually visitors. One super-rich family built a summer home that cost over a million dollars. The interior was completed by European craftspersons. Another super-rich visitor has a helicopter on the deck of his yacht. The "helicopter yacht" is a source of amusement to many islanders, but visibly irritates some visiting yacht owners who cannot match this level of conspicuous consumption.

The island seems to attract people with strong convictions and unique personalities. Many of them felt out of place in other communities, but they have found an amicable environment here. The freedom available in this community frequently enables them to pursue their unique aspirations. Most of them seem to blend into the community, but a few behave in a manner designed to attract attention. Eccentric or conspicuous behavior is not well regarded here, so those who quietly pursue their dreams are more likely to be respected in the community.

LOCAL CUSTOMS

Most islanders take a very casual approach to life, a factor that makes the island so appealing. Visitors should be aware, though, that many islanders are very serious about some issues and visitors are encouraged to respect those points. A visitor who flaunts the local customs is often called a "tourist," or a "@#* tourist." Even the most obnoxious tourists are treated courteously, but they are respected only for the dollars they spend. A "visitor" who respects the local values is always welcome and will be encouraged to return.

The island culture is too complex to define in a few words, but casualness and modesty are central elements in the local value system. Casualness appears in the way people meet their friends, in the way they dress, and the way they conduct their personal life. Modesty is reflected in one's clothing, vehicle, speech and deportment. These two traits may explain the presence of so many old cars and pickups on island roads.

CLOTHING

Casual attire is the norm on the island. Tattered jeans, ratty T-shirts, and dirty jogging shoes are acceptable in many places. However, visitors will probably be more comfortable if they wear something a little nicer for a party, a dinner, or a church service. Neckties and high heels are rarely worn on the island. They are definitely expected for court appearances. (Islanders know the court is in session when a prominent local attorney is seen wearing a jacket and tie.) Neckties and high heels are appropriate for high class parties at the Yacht Club, though the neckties tend to disappear during warm weather. Dress at church services varies from denomination to denomination, but neckties and high heels are appropriate. Most Presbyterians and Episcopalians are well dressed for Sunday services, while Roman Catholics rarely wear heels or ties to church, except on Christmas and Easter. The members of the other denominations tend to fall between the extremes. Visitors should be aware that many islanders dislike the absence of clothing on adults. Men should wear a shirt, and button it, unless they are on the beach or in a boat. Bathing suits are not suitable for shopping, sightseeing, or meals. Except for children, shorts are not suitable for every occasion.

Summer and fall days are warm but the evenings are cool, so provide a sweater and a windbreaker for everyone, even in August. The summers are usually dry, but be prepared for showers. During the winter and spring, the weather is usually mild, but it can be cold, windy, and wet. A wool sweater and a warm, water-resistant jacket are essential. Sensible shoes are appropriate for every season.

GREETINGS

Visitors are often surprised to be greeted by complete strangers. The residents frequently greet visitors they encounter on the street or in the store. It is part of the informal friendliness of the island. If a stranger greets you, please smile and say hello. When driving on the island, many residents will wave to you. This is also part of the island culture; please respond with a wave.

ISLAND TIME

Many island residents take a very casual attitude about promptness, a custom known as "island time." Being thirty minutes late for dinner or an appointment is common, and some arrive even later. One resident was invited to a reception scheduled from 2 to 4 PM. She arrived at 4:30 and asked, "Gee, didn't anybody come to the party?"

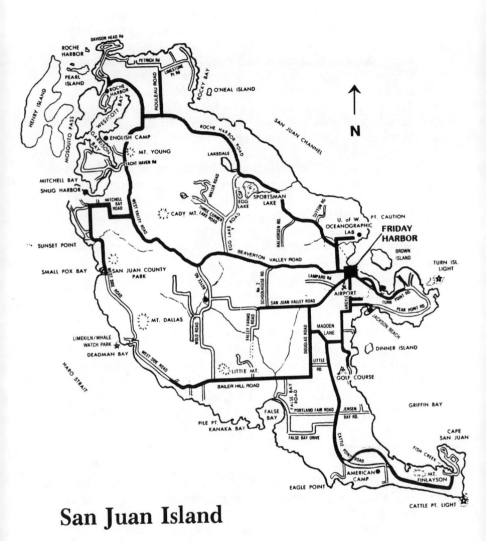

San Juan Island

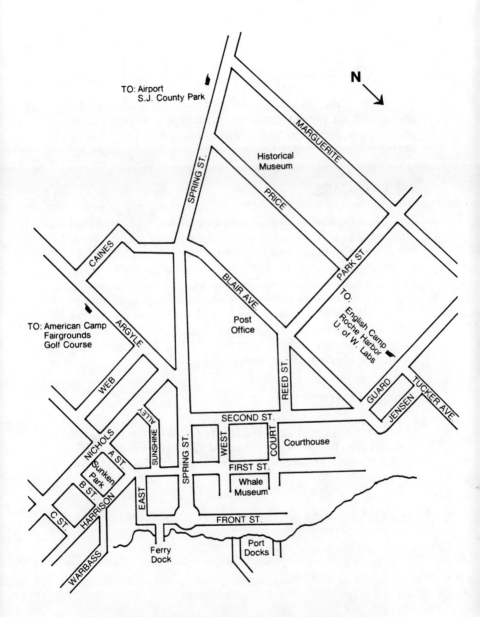

Friday Harbor, Washington

PRIVATE PROPERTY

Most residents tend to be very casual, but they resent trespassing on private property. Visitors should never enter private property without permission. Hunting on private property always requires written permission, which is frequently denied.

ISLAND CARS

Most residents demonstrate reverse snobbery about automobiles. A luxury sedan or a flashy sport car may be taboo, but a gray sedan from Japan is a high-prestige item. A pickup truck is an essential piece of equipment for the complete island gentleman. Many island families have two vehicles, a sedan for trips off the island and an older vehicle, usually a pickup, used on the island. The old car or pickup is called an "island car." A few dents and rust spots do not diminish its value, as it is rarely washed and never waxed. Visitors may think "island cars" are rolling junkheaps, but the residents cherish them.

SPEED LIMITS

The island speed limit is 45 MPH, with lower speeds posted in many areas. It is probably untrue that visitors receive more tickets than the residents, but visitors should observe the speed limit.

CHAPTER TWO:

MAJOR ANNUAL EVENTS

INDEPENDENCE DAY .... July 4th

Islanders have been celebrating Independence Day since 1859, when a few Americans gathered to raise a huge flag and hear speeches objecting to British oppression. The celebration later moved to Friday Harbor, where the day is celebrated with a parade, picnic, and fireworks. The parade begins at about 11:00 AM at the upper end of Spring St. The parade moves down Spring St. and ends at Sunken Park. It is followed by a picnic in the park. The Lions Club sells soft drinks and hot dogs in the park. Entertainment is provided by a local musical group and contests are offered for youngsters.

A fireworks display begins at dark. The fireworks are launched from a barge in the harbor and are visible throughout the harbor area. Another fireworks display is held at Roche Harbor.

Make hotel and motel reservations early. The ferries are crowded, so consider leaving your vehicle in Anacortes and traveling to the island as a foot passenger. Make airline reservations early

For additional information call   (206) 378-2240

JAZZ FESTIVAL .... .Last full weekend in July

This is the biggest annual event on the island, featuring a dozen jazz bands. The events are scheduled on Friday, Saturday, and Sunday and are held simultaneously in four locations. Admission badges purchased for the day or the weekend are honored at all locations.

Food and beverages are available at all locations. Make hotel and motel reservations early. Space for recreational vehicles is available at the fair grounds. Because of the crowds, you may have to wait six to eight hours to load an automobile on the ferry during the festival and the day after the festival. Consider traveling on the ferry as a foot passenger. Extra parking and a shuttle bus service is available in Anacortes. Shuttle bus service is available on the island. San Juan Airlines schedules extra flights, but make reservations early.

For additional information call (206) 378-2240

THE COUNTY FAIR . . . .The third weekend in August

This is an old-fashioned county fair in which islanders exhibit horses, cows, goats, sheep, chickens, rabbits, eggs, flowers, vegetables, fruit, canned goods, arts, crafts, clothing, etc. The county 4-H clubs judge several types of animals and homemaking projects. Equestrian competitions are conducted for youngsters. Islanders compete fiercely for the blue ribbons, which are a cherished possession in many island homes.

The biggest event at the fair is the Sheep-to-Shawl Contest, which features teams from Orcas, Lopez, and San Juan Islands. The contest begins with shearing a sheep, spinning the wool, then weaving a wool shawl. Points are awarded for the elapsed time and the quality of the work. This contest is closely watched by local folks who comment about the speed and skill of the contestants. Visitors are often fascinated by these ancient crafts. After watching a sheep being sheared, one youngster excitedly shouted, "Grandma, Grandma, we saw a man shave a pig." Her father turned pink and muttered, "There aren't many sheep in Seattle".

A fair official is on hand throughout the contest to explain the event to visitors.

Another event at the fair is the Chicken Race. Chickens of all types are entered, including anything the owner chooses to identify as "a chicken." Some odd-looking fowl frequently win the race. Burrell Osburn, the former County Extension Agent, is famous for entering unique "chickens" in the race.

For additional information call   (206) 378-4310

ROUND SHAW RACE . . . . Second Saturday in August

Several sailing regatta are held throughout the year, even in the winter, but the Round Shaw Race is the major sailing event of the year. The race is conducted by the San Juan Island Yacht Club but anyone may enter upon paying a modest fee. Boats are divided into several classes, based on size and configuration. The rules are casual and enforced on an honor basis. The race begins at Friday Harbor, goes around nearby Shaw Island in either direction and returns to Friday Harbor. Most sailors pack a light lunch, ample beverages, and a package of balloons. The balloons are filled with water and thrown at sailors in nearby boats. Sailors love the race but the ferry captains dread it. The race is conducted in the same narrow channels used by the ferries, frequently delaying the ferries on a busy weekend. People without boats can watch the start of the race from the bluff at the University of Washington Marine Laboratory.

For additional information call   (206) 378-5426

LIBRARY BOOK SALE . . . . . . A Saturday in July or August

The Friends of the San Juan Island Library conduct an annual book sale at the old high school gymnasium. Thousands of donated books are sold by the inch. Many readers bring large boxes and bags and stand in line to enter the gymnasium the mo-

9

ment the doors open. The profits support library services, especially services to children.

For additional information call   (206) 378-2798

WINTER EVENTS

Visitors often ask, "What do you do here in the winter?" The season is filled with many activities. Serious golfers, boaters, beach walkers, bird watchers, and tennis players continue these activities throughout the year. The fishing is excellent and many island residents participate in fishing derbies. A fishing derby "ladder" is posted in the window of the hardware store and it is closely watched to see who caught the biggest salmon.

The weather tends to be damp and dark and little commercial entertainment is available to fill the evenings and weekends. A few "snow birds" move to warmer climates till spring, but the snow birds and summer visitors miss a period when the social life of the community hits its peak. Nearly every church and social organization schedules one or more winter events. Private parties are held throughout the winter. Many residents devote the damp days of winter to playing bridge, visiting neighbors, reading books, writing poetry, pursuing hobbies, and participating in volunteer services at the library, the schools, the churches, and the Senior Citizens Center.

The cultural life of the community also hits its peak during the winter. The community hosts two professionally-directed music and theater groups. The San Juan Singers present winter and spring concerts and the Straights of Juan de Fuca present plays and operettas throughout the year. Winter is also a time for classes and lectures offered by the community college, the library, and other organizations. The staff of the San Juan Island Library is busy supplying books, videocassettes, and audio cassettes for winter enjoyment. The library's storytelling, reading, and craft programs are popular with children.

The Christmas season begins when the Santa Ship arrives early in December. The ship is operated by the Canadian Forces Reserves. Santa is a retired Canadian Forces Chief Petty Officer. He has a big heart, a hearty laugh, a full beard, and a sturdy physique well suited for his role. The brightly decorated ship arrives at about 6 PM and Santa and his friends emerge to greet the children and adults. Santa then rides a fire truck to the nursing home, where he greets the staff and residents. While Santa is at the nursing home, the children and adults troop to the high school gymnasium where Santa visits each child and gives each one a toy and an orange.

The Christmas Committee decorates the town for the season. On a Saturday in December, members of the Lions, Kiwanis, American Legion, Scouts, Chamber of Commerce, Youth Dynamics, and others decorate the marina, the ferry dock, and the business district. A large Christmas tree and a creche are installed at the intersection of Spring and Argyle Sts. That evening, friends gather to see the lights lit and hear seasonal music sung by the San Juan Singers. The lighting ceremony is followed by cocoa, cider, and cookies at the National Park Headquarters.

A few days before Christmas, the Posada, a Mexican Christmas story, is enacted on the streets of Friday Harbor. Mary, Joseph, and a "mule" travel through the streets, accompanied by many children and adults. They stop at several places where Joseph requests a room for himself and his wife. He is repeatedly refused--then finally finds a willing host at a local church. After being accepted, Mary, Joseph, and those who accompanied them enter the church to sing Christmas hymns and hear the Christmas story read from Sacred Scripture. This is followed by snacks in the church social hall and pinata breaking by the little ones. (Someone usually takes an apple to the "mule".) The Posada is sponsored by the Episcopal, Catholic, and Presbyterian churches, who take turns hosting the event.

New Year's Eve and New Year's Day are celebrated with many private parties. After that, the social whirl subsides, but does not end. Most island residents raise fruit, flowers, and vegetables, so many dark days after Christmas are devoted to examining seed and nursery catalogs and planning an early start on the garden.

OTHER EVENTS

Many events are scheduled on short notice and cannot be identified here. Information about these events are listed in the local weekly newspapers. Information also can be obtained from the tourist information number, (206) 378-2240.

CHAPTER THREE:

LOCAL FACILITIES

LODGING

BED & BREAKFASTS: All but one are old homes that have been restored. They provide a pleasant bedroom, a shared bath, and an excellent breakfast. The B&B's in Friday Harbor are within walking distance of several restaurants.

In Friday Harbor:
Blair House .... Phone (206) 378-2506

Collins House .... Phone (206) 378-5834

Tucker House .... Phone (206) 378-2783

Wharfside B&B .... Phone (206) 378-5661

In the country:
Duffy House .... Phone (206) 378-5604

Moon & Sixpence .... Phone (206) 378-4138

Olympic Lights .... Phone (206) 378-3186

The Meadows .... Phone (206) 378-4004

HOTELS: These nineteenth century hotels have been modernized and most of the rooms are furnished with antiques.

Hotel de Haro .... Phone (206) 378-2155

    A small hotel at Roche Harbor Resort

.San Juan Inn .... Phone (206) 378-2070

    A small hotel near the Friday Harbor waterfront

MOTELS: Modern units located in Friday Harbor.

Friday Harbor Motor Inn .... Phone (206) 378-4351

Island Lodge .... Phone (206) 378-2000

    HOSTEL: A small nineteenth century hotel in Friday Harbor that operates like a European hostel.

Elite Hotel .... Phone (206) 378-5555

    RESORTS:

Lonesome Cove Resort .... Phone (206) 378-4477

Mar Vista Resort .... Phone (206) 378-4448

Roche Harbor Resort .... Phone (206) 378-2155

CAMPGROUNDS

San Juan County Park, 380 West Side Rd., Phone (206) 378-2992. Tent camping and RV hookups.

Lakedale Campground, 2627 Roche Harbor Rd., Phone (206) 378-2350. Tent camping and RV hookups.

Town & Country Mobile Home Park, 595 Tucker Ave., Phone (206) 378-4717, RV hookups.

Camping is prohibited in the national parks. RV parking is available at the fair grounds during the Jazz Festival.

GOLF COURSE

The San Juan Golf & Country Club is open to the public. Clubs and carts may be rented in the pro shop. Lunch is served daily in the summer, and on selected days in the off season. Phone (206) 378-2254.

From downtown Friday Harbor, drive 1.5 miles on Argyle Ave., then .7 miles on Golf Course Rd. (The intersection of Argyle Ave. and Golf Course Rd. is on a curve and is poorly marked.)

MUSEUMS

San Juan Island Historical Museum

405 Price St. Phone (206) 378-4587. Open Memorial Day through Labor Day, Wednesday-Saturday, 1:00-4:00 pm and by appointment the rest of the year. The museum is described in page 65.

The Whale Museum

62 First St. N. Phone (206) 378-4710 or (800)-562-8832 Open 11 to 4, daily. The museum is described on page 101.

ART GALLERIES

Atelier Gallerie

Cabezon Gallery, 60 First St.

Islands Own, Cannery Landing

Raven House Art, 1 Spring St.

Reid Gallery, 185 First St.

Sunshine Gallery (artists' coop), 110 Sunshine Alley

Trumpeters, 435 Argyle St.

Waterworks Gallery, 315 Argyle St.

LIBRARY

San Juan Island Library, 1010 Guard St. Phone (206) 378-2798. Open: Tues., Wed., Fri., & Sat. 11 to 6; Thur. 11 to 9.

PARKS

San Juan Island National Historic Park

Office, 125 Spring St.Phone (206) 378-2240

English Camp is described on page 78.

American Camp is described on page 51.

San Juan County Park. The park is on the west side of the island and is described on page 81.

Lime Kiln/Whale Watch park is on the west side of the island and is described on page 82.

Sunken Park is one block up the hill from the ferry terminal. It has picnic tables and drinking water. Restrooms are available in the ferry terminal, a block away. Limited parking is available on the streets around the park.

The Port District Waterfront Park overlooks the marina. From the bottom of Spring St., take the sidewalk along the shore going toward the marina (away from the ferry terminal). Drinking water and restrooms are available at the nearby Port District Office. Limited parking is available on nearby streets and the Port District parking lot.

Circle Park is a thumbnail-sized park at the bottom of Spring St., overlooking the harbor. It has benches, but no picnic tables. Drinking water and restrooms are available at the ferry terminal, a block away. Limited parking is available on nearby streets.

West Street Park is a small park at the end of West St. overlooking the harbor. From the waterfront, go up Spring St., then turn right on First St. Go one block on First St., then turn right on West St. The park is at the end of the block. Picnic tables are available but drinking water and restrooms are not available. The town hopes to renovate this park soon. Limited parking is available on nearby streets.

Jackson Beach is a popular park 1.3 miles from downtown Friday Harbor. Picnic tables, drinking water, and restrooms are NOT available. The park is described on page 108.

PUBLIC RESTROOMS

From 1924 through 1927, the American Legion Auxiliary maintained public restrooms in the old American Legion Hall, near the corner of Spring and Argyle Sts. The Auxiliary's 1927 annual report indicated it was forced to close the restrooms due to cost and the "lack of appreciation by the general public." In 1934, the Commercial Club petitioned the Town of Friday Harbor to build public restrooms near the waterfront. In recent years, the Chamber of Commerce has repeatedly urged the Town and the Port of Friday Harbor to build public restrooms, but the funds have not been available.

Public restrooms are available on the waterfront in the ferry terminal and on the ground floor at the Port of Friday Harbor office (a block from Circle Park). On Second St., public restrooms are available in the Town Hall and the Courthouse.

PUBLIC TRANSPORTATION

FERRY: Ferry service to the island is provided by the Washington State Ferries, to Anacortes, WA and Sidney, BC, with intermediate stops at Orcas, Lopez, and Shaw Islands.

Anacortes--Friday Harbor: Reservations are not available, so passengers must wait in line to board the ferries. If you leave your car and travel as a foot passenger, you are almost always assured of boarding the next ferry. Bicycles are given preference in loading and are usually not delayed by heavy traffic. If you plan to bring a car to the island, get in line well before the departure time. During the winter, a thirty minute wait may be sufficient. In the summer, two hours is usually sufficient, except on busy days. Traffic from Anacortes to Friday Harbor is heavy on Fridays and Saturdays, and on Thursdays before three-day weekends. The traffic from Friday Harbor to Anacortes is heavy on Sunday afternoons and Monday mornings. Four to six hour waits are not uncommon on summer weekends. Six hour delays are typical during major holidays. For information, phone (206) 378-4777 or (800)-542-0810.

Friday Harbor--Sidney, BC: The ferries to Canada dock at Sidney, British Columbia, sixteen miles north of Victoria. The ferries usually make one trip a day between Friday Harbor and Sidney. Reservations are available during the tourist season. Make reservation several days in advance at the Anacortes, Friday Harbor, or Sidney ferry terminals. For information or reservations, phone (206) 378-4777 or (800)-542-0810.

Some of the best sightseeing in the islands is available from the upper decks of the ferries. Bald eagles are frequently seen

21

perching in dead trees or circling in the sky. With luck, you may see porpoise or whales. Food and beverage service is available on the ferries, or you may bring a lunch.

Belairco, Inc. has announced plans for a passenger-only ferry service between Squalicum Harbor in Bellingham and the Port of Friday Harbor. When the route application is approved, the service will operate from about June 1 to mid-September. The boat will carry 49 passengers, 18 bicycles, and a few kayaks. For information, phone (206) 733-9440.

AIRLINE: San Juan Airlines began in Friday Harbor in 1947 with a single-engine plane operating from a pasture near town. Today, it is a modern commuter airline flying twin-engine aircraft to Seattle, Portland, Bellingham, and Vancouver. The aircraft fly at 2,500 to 3,500 feet altitude and the views are spectacular. Phone United Airlines, at 800-241-6522, for information or reservations.

Lake Union Air operates single-engine float planes from Seattle and Victoria to Friday Harbor and Roche Harbor. Phone (800)-692-9223 or (206)-284-0300 for information or reservations.

TRANSIT BUS: During the tourist season, San Juan Tour and Transit offers bus service to Lakedale, Roche Harbor, English Camp, Whale Watch Park, American Camp, and other points on the island. The van departs hourly from the airport and the bottom of Spring St. Phone (206) 378-5545.

Evergreen Trailways offers daily bus service between the Anacortes ferry terminal and the Seattle bus terminals, with connections to Seattle-Tacoma International Airport. Evergreen Trailways also offers daily bus service between the Sidney ferry terminal and downtown Victoria. Tickets may be purchased on the ferry from the bus driver. In Victoria, purchase tickets from the driver. In Seattle, purchase tickets at either bus terminal. For information, phone (206) 626-6090.

GUIDED TOURS

BUS TOURS: San Juan Tour and Transit offers narrated tours of the island operating hourly from the airport and the bottom of Spring St. On request, the driver meets guests at their home, motel, or inn. Phone (206) 378-5545.

Friday Harbor Motor Inn offers narrated tours on a double-decker bus. The bus makes two or three trips a day, departing from the inn's parking lot. Phone (206) 378-4351.

BOAT TOURS: Western Prince Wildlife Tours depart five days a week from the marina in Friday Harbor. The tours emphasize whales, eagles, and other wildlife. The narration is provided by a naturalist. Phone (206) 378-5315.

Grayline boat tours depart daily from Semiahmo Inn, near Blaine WA. and stop in Friday Harbor. Phone (206) 371-5222.

CHARTER BOATS: Two fishing and sightseeing boats operate from the Port of Friday Harbor:

Buffalo Works, Capt. Bob Brittain, PO Box 478, Friday Harbor, WA 98250, Phone (206) 378-4612.

Captain Clyde's Charters, Capt. Clyde Rice, PO Box 1212, Friday Harbor, WA 98250, Phone (206) 378-3404.

GREAT PLACES FOR KIDS

San Juan Island is an ideal place for kids to see and study whales. During the summer, whales are frequently seen at Whale

Watch Park, on the west side of the island. **CAUTION: Children require close supervision near the cliffs at the Whale Watch Park.** Addiional information appears on pages 94-95.

The Whale Museum in Friday Harbor is the only museum in the US devoted to the natural history of living whales. It includes many interesting exhibits suitable for children and adults. The Museum is on First St., two blocks above Spring St. It is open from 11 am to 4 pm, daily.

There are times when kids need to run, and play, and let off steam. The following places are reasonably safe, but adult supervision is necessary.

Sunken Park in Friday Harbor is one block up the hill from the ferry terminal. It has basketball goals, a skateboard "tube", and a lawn for play. This is a great place for kids to play while waiting for the ferry or waiting for adults to return from shopping.

Jackson Beach, 1.3 miles from Friday Harbor, is convenient for picnics and playing. More information is on page 108.

The best playground is South Beach, ten miles from Friday Harbor, at the American Camp National Park. It has a sandy beach, abundant driftwood, picnic tables, fire pits, and restrooms. More information begins on page 56.

If South Beach is too windy, try the American Camp Picnic Ground, two miles away. From South Beach, go up the paved road to the stop sign. Turn left and watch for a small sign identifying the picnic area. More information is on page 61.

LIVE MUSIC

Live music is available almost every weekend. The times, places, and performers are identified in the weekly newspapers.

The Jazz Festival is held the last full weekend of July. Well-known artists from around the country perform at the festival.

SERVICE CLUBS

The Kiwanis Club meets Thursday noons at Mojo's Restaurant.

The Lions Club meets Tuesday noons in the American Legion.

CROSSING THE INTERNATIONAL BORDER

US and Canada have a long history of cooperation so crossing the international border is relatively easy. Although visas and passports are not required, suitable identification must be available to immigration and customs agents. A driver's license is helpful, but a voter-registration certificate, passport, military ID, or other document identifying citizenship or residency is preferred.

Canada denies entrance to visitors carrying handguns. Handguns may be deposited for short periods with the Washington State Ferries or the San Juan County Sheriff. Border authorities seize many fresh fruits and vegetables carried across the border. To be safe, buy fruit and vegetables after crossing the border. Dogs and cats need a health certificate from a veterinarian showing the animals are vaccinated for rabies.

Both countries allow their citizens to bring a limited value of merchandise into the country without paying duties. Check with the customs agent of your country for the current regulations.

The exchange rate between the US and Canadian dollar changes daily. Businesses on San Juan Island accept Canadian currency at close to the current exchange rate.

ORCA OR KILLER WHALES

Orca or Killer Whales are numerous around San Juan Island and are frequently seen during June, July, and August. They are not fish, but mammals. They breath air and give birth to live infants who are nursed by their mothers. Newborn calves begin swimming immediately after birth, but they remain near their mothers for up to two years. Mothers are assisted in caring for their calves by a related female, usually an immature sibling, an aunt, or a grandmother. The calves are are almost always seen in the company of two females. Orca live in "pods" consisting of an extended family of three to fifty whales.

Mature males are up to thirty feet long and weigh up to four tons; mature females are about one third smaller. Mature males can be identified by a large dorsal fin which can be as much as six feet high, which is much larger than the dorsal fins on females and immature males. Scientists identify individual orca by the size, color, and shape of the dorsal fin and the "saddle patch," a pigmented area near the dorsal fin. Orca are powerful swimmers. Jacques Cousteau discovered they could swim thirty- five miles per hour in short bursts. They can dive deeply, but must surface within a few minutes to breath.

The name "killer whales" was given to them by whalers who saw Orca attack and eat other warm-blooded animals, especially dolphins, seals, and smaller whales. Two or three Orca sometimes attack much larger whales, though the larger whales frequently resist the attack. Orca living in Puget and Washington Sounds primarily eat fish. The transient pods are more likely to eat warm-blooded animals. Orca almost never attack humans, and then only when severely provoked.

CHAPTER FOUR:

A THUMBNAIL HISTORY OF

SAN JUAN ISLAND

The Northwest Indians used the island as a summer home for several centuries. Some Indians spent the winters in large villages on the mainland. Each spring, they dispersed to many small villages to gather food for the winter. Several summer villages stood in the sheltered bays on the south and west sides of the island. A few Indian villages on the island were occupied year round. Carbon dating indicates some of them were several centuries old. A few were in use at the turn of the century.

While living on the island, the men fished, hunted, and gathered clams while the women and slaves gathered roots, nuts, and berries and preserved the food for winter. Fish were caught in reef nets made of vines. The nets were strung between two anchored canoes over a reef and allowed to settle to the bottom. When a school of salmon passed over the reef, the net was quickly raised, sometimes trapping hundreds of salmon in a single catch. (Early European and American settlers adopted reef-net fishing and it is still used by a few commercial fishermen.) The women and slaves dried the fish on racks in the sun, then smoked them in the longhouse so they would keep for a year or more.

Garrison Bay, at English Camp, served as a summer trading post for Indians from several hundred miles to the north and south. Trade items included arrows, spear heads, shells, jewelry, blankets, nuts, berries, and other commodities. After the Hudson Bay Co. opened trading posts in the area, the Indians began trading salmon, furs, and blankets in exchange for guns, gunpowder, knives, axes, whiskey, and beads.

Each Autumn, most of the Indians gathered their possessions and moved to a central community on the mainland. Thousands of Indians spent the winters in the large communities, visiting, trading, and fulfilling ritual obligations. A few Indians remained on the island all year.

The island was discovered by Europeans in 1592. The navigator on that trip was Apostolos Valerianos, a Greek who was known to the Spanish as Juan de Fuca. Valerianos was a skilled navigator who hypothesized that a northwest passage between the Atlantic and Pacific should be found in this area. The Spanish fleet under his leadership found the straits between the Olympic Peninsula and Vancouver Island and assumed it was the entrance to the northwest passage. The fleet spent twenty days exploring the straits and adjoining waters. Several subsequent exploring expeditions failed to find the straits, and many assumed Valerianos was mistaken about its presence. Valerianos' discovery was verified in 1790 by a Spanish expedition led by Lt. Francisco Eliza. Eliza gave San Juan Island its name, a shortened version of the name of Valerianos' sponsor, Don Juan Vincente de Guemes Pacheco de Padilla Horcasitees y Aguayo, who was also known as Conde Revilla. Revilla was the Viceroy of Mexico who sent Valerianos to find the Northwest Passage.

THE PIG WAR

The island's great claim to fame arose from a minor territorial dispute between the US and Great Britain. The western part of the US-Canadian border was established by the Treaty of 1846. The border between Lake of the Woods in Minnesota and Vancouver Island was set at the 49th parallel. To protect Hudson Bay Co. interests, the treaty placed the border in the channel between Vancouver Island and the mainland. Early residents discovered there were two major channels between the island and the mainland. The Hudson Bay Co. started Bellevue Farm to establish a legal precedent to ownership of the disputed area. This dispute led to the Pig War of 1859. It began in 1858 when unsuccessful gold miners from the Fraser and Thompson River gold fields began settling on the island. Most of the island was covered with trees, so they chose open land on the south side of the island. Some of the first to arrive were Lyman A. Cutler and Henry Webber, who chose ground on the sheep pastures of Bellevue Farm. Cutler was a tall, slender young man from Ohio who had a reputation for being lazy, hot tempered, and a skillful marksman. He chose ground about a mile and a half northwest of the Bellevue Farm buildings, where he built a small log cabin for himself and a young Indian woman. Charles J. Griffin, the farm manager, complained that Cutler was trespassing on Hudson Bay Co. property and asked him to leave. Cutler insisted the British were trespassing on US territory, and refused to move. Cutler bought a peck of potatoes in Sequim and planted them for a cash crop. He built a rudimentary fence around his potato patch, but a big black boar from Bellevue Farm penetrated the fence and began eating the potatoes. Cutler chased the boar home several times and complained to Griffin about the damage. Although Griffin was firm in protecting Hudson Bay Company's rights, he was not without compassion. On at least one occasion he helped Cutler improve the fence to keep the boar out of the potatoes. However, having tasted the potatoes, the boar continued to penetrate the fence to enjoy a juicy meal. Early on the morning of June 15, 1859, Jacob, a Black servant at Bellevue Farm, rode by Cutler's cabin. He laughed when he saw the boar rooting in Cutler's potato patch. His laughter awakened Cutler, who seized his rifle and shot the boar. Cutler may have had second thoughts about his rash act, as he promptly went to Griffin and offered ten dollars in compensation for the boar. If that was not satisfactory, Cutler offered to exchange one of his own pigs for the dead animal. The usually amicable Griffin lost his temper and demanded one hundred dollars for the boar. Since mature pigs commonly sold for six to ten dollars, Cutler declined. Cutler suggested that a panel of three neighbors establish the value of the dead animal, but Griffin refused. Intemperate remarks were exchanged.

That afternoon, three Hudson Bay Co. officials who were visiting the island went to Cutler's cabin to persuade him to pay one hundred dollars for the pig. When Cutler refused, they threatened to arrest him and have him tried in Victoria. Cutler picked up his rifle--then slammed the door in their faces. The officials withdrew to reconsider. After they left, Cutler discussed the matter with Paul K. Hubbs, the US Customs Collector. Upon discussing the matter with other Americans, Hubbs rowed to the mainland to mail a report of the events to his superior, Morris Frost. Hubbs also discussed it with an old friend, Capt. George E. Pickett. Pickett promised to report the matter to his superior, Brig. Gen. William S. Harney, the Army commander for the Oregon Territory.

While he was at Bellingham Bay, Hubbs bought a large US flag. On July 4, 1859, fourteen US citizens gathered to raise the flag, fire their guns, and hear fourteen speeches condemning British oppression of US citizens. On July 8, Gen. Harney visited the island to discuss the problem with Hubbs. Harney asked Hubbs to draft a statement requesting Army protection for the island. The statement did not mention the pig, but stressed the need for protection from Indians. The statement was signed by all the Americans on the island. Harney did not wait to receive the statement, but immediately dispatched Pickett's 9th Infantry, Company D to occupy the island. Pickett and about sixty soldiers arrived at Griffin Bay on July 26, 1859, on the *USS Massachusetts*.

When James Douglas, now the governor of the Province Victoria, learned of the military occupation of the island, he sent Maj. John Fitzroy de Courcy to Griffin Bay to arrest Cutler and establish a British military presence. Maj. de Courcy arrived the evening of July 26, 1859, a few hours after the U.S. Army arrived on the island. Hubbs anticipated the British plans so he arrested Cutler in the name of the United States government. While Hubbs and his prisoner were walking through the forest to the US Army

31

camp, they met Maj. de Courcy and three British officers traveling toward Cutler's cabin. Words were exchanged, but the Americans were not detained. Cutler remained at the Army camp for a few days before his friends persuaded him to hide till the issue was resolved.

That day, Capt. Pickett issued a proclamation entitled "Orders, No. 1." Among other things it stated:

> This being United States territory, no laws, other than those of the United States, nor courts, except such as are held by virtue of said laws, will be recognized or allowed on this island.

When the British read this document they returned to Victoria to report the events to Gov. James Douglas. The next day, on July 28, the British frigate *Tribune* entered Griffin Bay and brought its guns to bear on the American military camp. Pickett then requested assistance from his commander, Lt. Col. Silas Casey. The matter had been arranged in advance and Casey immediately dispatched the *Massachusetts* with a detachment of infantry under the direction of Maj Granville Haller. Douglas responded by dispatching *Plumper* with a detachment of royal engineers and light infantry. Pickett, with about sixty men and three small brass cannon, was outnumbered by sixty-one heavy naval guns and 775 men. Pickett prepared to resist a landing, but when Haller arrived, Pickett declined his assistance. One historian suggests Pickett declined because he did not want to surrender the command to a senior officer.

The British commander, Cap. Geoffrey Phipps Hornby, received orders from Douglas to proceed cautiously in this matter. Pickett and Hornby met at the American camp on August 3rd. Hornby urged a joint occupation of the island until the diplomats could resolve the issue. Pickett rejected his offer. Hornby then announced that he was instructed to land and planned to do so immediately. Pickett responded that he would resist the superior British force "as long as I have a man." Then, privately, he asked Hornby if he would delay his landing by forty-eight hours so he could request further orders from Harney. "Not one minute," Hornby answered. Upon returning to his ship, Hornby reread his orders and delayed his landing. His decision undoubtedly prevented serious bloodshed.

Upon receiving Pickett's request for assistance, Harney ordered all the troops under his command to go immediately to San Juan Island. Casey crowded three infantry companies on *Julia*, an old sternwheel mail boat, and rushed to the scene. They arrived the morning of August 10th, but the US Army was still outnumbered. As soon as his troops were in position, Casey invited Hornby to come ashore to arrange a meeting with Hornby's superior, Rear Adm. R.L. Baynes. The meeting was arranged; Baynes refused to meet Casey, but he gave Hornby orders to avoid bloodshed. Meanwhile, Haller arrived from quelling an Indian uprising and the guns of the *Massachusetts* were moved to earthen fortifications at the crest of the ridge. (The fortifications were designed by Lt. Henry M. Robert, a recent graduate of the Military Academy. Robert later became the commander of the Army Engineers, but is better known as the author of *Robert's Rules of Order).* Casey drew troops, guns, and supplies from military installations throughout Puget Sound in an unsuccessful effort to equalize the strength of the contending forces.

Douglas and Baynes faced a quandary. Their occupation of the island appeared legally correct until the boundary dispute could be resolved through a treaty. The British military forces were probably stronger than the American forces, but Vancouver Island was crowded with armed Americans who were eager for a fight. Furthermore, in a prolonged conflict, the Americans would have little difficulty disrupting British supply line from England. Although the Americans were eager to fight, Baynes ordered his ships to maintain their position, but "not on any account whatever [to] take the initiative in commencing hostilities."

The US War Department was displeased that Harney occupied the island without orders. He was told to inform the British that the island was occupied only to suppress Indian problems and it was not intended to prejudge the boundary issue. Lt. Gen. Winfield Scott, the General in Chief of the Army, was immediately sent to Washington Territory to establish a joint military occupation of the island until the issue could be resolved. Douglas opposed a joint occupation, but he was overruled by the British ambassador in Washington.

The following spring, Capt. George Bazelgette and one hundred Royal Marines landed on the island. The Royal Marines remained from March, 1860 until October, 1872. During the twelve year occupation, the British officers and enlisted men became good friends with their American counterparts. They entertained each other handsomely on every opportunity. The Americans entertained the British on Independence Day and the British reciprocated on Queen Victoria's Birthday.

The boundary dispute was settled by the Treaty of Washington of 1871, which concentrated on fishing rights and damages to the US by British-built gunboats sold to the Confederacy. The San Juan Island boundary dispute was a secondary issue. The parties could not agree on the boundary, so they agreed to arbitration by Kaiser Wilhelm I of Germany. The Emperor appointed a panel of geographers to recommend a decision. US Ambassador George Bancroft met the panel and built a strong case for the US position. After a lengthy review, the panel recommended, by a two-to-one vote, that the US position be upheld. On October 21, 1872, the Emperor announced that the boundary should be in the center of Haro Straits. The news reached the San Juans in November and the Americans celebrated for several days.

The Royal Marines transferred their camp to the US Army on November 25, 1872. As a part of the decommissioning ceremony, the Union Jack was lowered, then the flagpole was taken down and sawed in pieces. A small piece was given to each Marine and a large piece was taken to the naval dock at Esquimalt, which the Americans interpreted as a calculated insult. They erected a temporary flagpole and raised the Stars and Stripes. A small US Army contingent occupied the British camp until 1874, when the Army withdrew from the island.

Most British citizens, including some ex-Marines, remained on the island. Within two weeks, seventy-four British citizens in the San Juans filed for US citizenship to protect their land claims. Most of those claims were eventually honored.

When the U.S. Army arrived in July, 1859, there were twenty-two U.S. citizens on the island. They were all men and most of them were out-of-luck gold miners. When the dispute was settled in 1872, the island was populated by a few hundred people. Most lived on farms in the San Juan Valley and the adjoining areas of the island, where they produced most of their own food and clothing. They raised small cash crops to pay for tobacco, liquor, sugar, coffee, gunpowder, and other necessities. A few residents worked in small lime quarries. The children attended a one-room school a few months each summer until they mastered the rudiments of reading, writing, and arithmetic. After that, they worked for their parents or for a neighbor. As the population grew, the forests were cleared and much of the island was used for farming. Some farms had herds of sheep while others had herds of milk cows. Some residents supplemented their income by smuggling wool, Chinese immigrants, liquor, and other contraband from Canada. Due to high import taxes, wool could be purchased cheaply in Canada and sold at a profit in the US. The wool smugglers mixed imported wool with the wool from their own sheep to avoid detection. Government statistics reveal that sheep in San Juan County produced almost twice as much wool as sheep in other counties. Immigrants from China were smuggled into the US to circumvent the Chinese Exclusion Act of 1882. When the Volstead Act passed in 1919, local smugglers imported large quantities of liquor from Canada. Most of it was reshipped to other parts of the country.

FRIDAY HARBOR

The town of Friday Harbor did not exist during the Pig War. In 1858, fourteen years before the town was formed, Capt. G.H. Richards of the Royal Navy was assigned to survey the area. Richards gave names to many geographic features which are still used today. He named the harbor, Friday Harbor, but he did not explain his reason for doing so. He probably named it for Joe Friday, who lived near the present University of Washington Marine Laboratory.

Joe Friday was a Kanaka, a name given to men from Hawaii who worked in Australia, North America, and elsewhere. His real name is unknown; he was named Joe Friday by his employers who did not want to use his Polynesian name. Friday may have been taken from a Polynesian character in Daniel Defoe's, *The Life and Strange Surprizing Adventures of Robinson Crusoe.* The novel was published in 1719 and was popular during the nineteenth century. A family history reports that he was shipwrecked and saved his life by clinging to a chicken coop till it washed ashore. He served for several years as the manager of Hudson Bay Co. Sheep Station No. 2, near the harbor. When the Hudson Bay Co. abandoned its property claims on the island, Friday was not a US citizen so he could not claim the land, but he continued raising sheep there. He married an Indian woman and their descendants lived on the island until recently.

In 1873, the year after the boundary issue was resolved, the state legislature created San Juan County. The new county was separated from Whatcom County and encompassed the area that had been in dispute with Great Britain. Capt. Edward D. Warbass, the former sutler (storekeeper) at American Camp, was appointed the first Auditor. Warbass decided a new county seat should be established at Friday Harbor. He exercised a clause in

36

the law which allowed the county to claim 160 acres of land for official use. Warbass built a sixteen by twenty-four foot shack which served as the courthouse and his home. He had the town surveyed and offered lots for sale. Most residents lived on the south end of the island and preferred to shop at Israel Katz's store in San Juan Town. Warbass got a post office established in Friday Harbor in January 1876, but the weekly mail boat usually skipped Friday Harbor because it had no mail for the town. Warbass was not easily defeated, so he rode to Argyle once a week to mail a letter to himself. After that, the mail boat had to stop at Friday Harbor. In the three years Warbass was the Auditor, he failed to sell a single lot in Friday Harbor.

The next Auditor was John H. Bowman, the county's first Probate Judge. Bowman was a well-educated man who ran a farm and a private school on Orcas Island. Bowman shared Warbass' dream of building a new community in Friday Harbor. In 1876, Bowman bought fifty-six acres of county land, almost half of the county land for $176. He arranged to have the money deducted from his auditor's fees, as they were paid. Bowman's property faced the harbor and included a natural spring. Much of downtown Friday Harbor now stands in the Bowman tract.

Warbass was angry that the commissioners sold the property so cheaply and on such generous terms and promised never to live in Friday Harbor again. Warbass bought 110 acres along the waterfront east of Friday Harbor and formed a new town, named Idlewild. Warbass bought an officer's house at American Camp and had it moved to Idlewild. During his remaining years, Idlewild remained largely unpopulated except for Warbass and a US Revenue Launch Station. The road through Idlewild is now known as Warbass Lane. In 1904, Warbass sold Idlewild to Capt. Andrew Newhall, an Orcas Island lumber mill operator and ship owner. Warbass retained the right to live in his home for the rest of his life. He died on December 16, 1906.

Bowman sold about half of the county land to Joseph Sweeny, a prosperous Orcas Island storekeeper. People on Orcas Island thought Sweeny's wealth came from smuggling, but he was never charged with the crime. Sweeny cleared part of the land and built a store. Other island residents were not interested in the community so Sweeny, Bowman and the Friday family were the only residents for several years. The population declined when Joe Friday moved his family and sheep a few miles away. In desperation, Bowman and Sweeny gave lots to people to induce them to live in Friday Harbor. They could not sell lots till they lowered the price to twenty dollars for waterfront lots and ten dollars for other lots.

In 1882, William Douglas paid ten dollars for a building lot and built a competing general store across Spring St. from Sweeny's store. Douglas included a back room bar in his store. It was so popular that Sweeny put a bar in his store, too. Low prices for good whiskey and beer soon brought customers. It also gave Friday Harbor the reputation as the town built by the liquor trade.

Business at the two stores improved and people started buying lots. Bowman and Sweeny raised the price for vacant lots and people continued to buy them. In 1883, the county commissioners built a larger courthouse and sold Warbass' shanty to Israel Katz. Katz, who ran the store and bar at San Juan Town, recognized that Friday Harbor was growing, so he began a produce business in Friday Harbor. That same year, Katz bought a larger building to house the business. (The building still stands at the bottom of Spring St.) Katz's store at San Juan Town began dwindling as more and more islanders started drinking and shopping in Friday Harbor. On July 4, 1890, the Katz Store at San Juan Town burned down, then the Friday Harbor merchants and saloon keepers only had to compete with the Bergman Store at Argyle and a few stores on the west side of the island. In 1890, the Argyle Wagon Rd. was completed. (The old trails were too narrow for wagons, so the new road offered improved transportation between Friday Harbor and the south end of the island.)

The town got a boost in 1890 when the Friday Harbor Packing Co. opened. The packing plant processed thousands of cans of salmon each year. A second cannery opened a few years later. The Tacoma and Roche Harbor Lime Co. expanded in the 1890's, creating additional prosperity. Evidence of 1890's prosperity was visible in several new buildings, including a two-story school, the Tourists' Hotel, the Methodist Church, the Presbyterian Church, the Seventh-Day Adventist Church, and the Odd Fellows Lodge (all but the school are still standing.) During that period, several merchants built comfortable new homes at the edge of town. In 1890, the merchants Joseph and John Sweeny bought a large farm that became a showplace of modern agriculture.

Prosperity continued with occasional ups and downs until the late 1930's when the pea cannery closed and the nation-wide depression was felt locally, the local economy improved somewhat, but a major economic depression struck during the 1950's when farming, fishing, logging, and lime quarrying were depressed simultaneously. Unemployment was high and many residents left the island to find work. Some businesses closed and others had difficulty paying their bills. Building maintenance was deferred and the town became rather shabby.

The revival began early in the 1960's when investors bought several old business buildings and restored them under federal incentive programs. During the 1960's, the economy was spurred by an influx of retirees and a growth in tourism. The economy got a quick boost in 1966 when Friday Harbor and Roche Harbor served as locales for the film, *Namu the Killer Whale.* The growth was rapid in the 1970's and continued at a moderate rate in the 1980's.

ROCHE HARBOR

Roche Harbor, on the north end of the island, received its name from a splendid natural harbor named for Left Lt. Richard Roche, of the Royal Navy. During the joint military occupation, the Royal Marines discovered a limestone deposit at White Point, near Roche Harbor. The northern tip of the island contains the largest and purest limestone deposit west of the Mississippi. Lime is an essential ingredient for producing concrete, iron, and paper. The Marines were assigned to quarry and burn (process) lime, which was sold by the Hudson Bay Co. After the British left in 1872, Robert and Richard Scurr filed a claim on the property and continued quarrying and burning lime under the name of White Point Lime Co. In 1886, they sold their property for $40,000 to John Stafford McMillan, a 31-year-old attorney from Tacoma. McMillan and a few partners formed the Tacoma and Roche Harbor Lime Co. The Scurr brothers remained on the island and operated a 183 acre farm near Roche Harbor, where they grew hay, sheep, and apples.

McMillan was a large, dynamic man who inherited wealth from his parents and married the daughter of a wealthy man. He was not content to live on inherited wealth but entertained major financial ambitions. He ran the company and the town as his personal fiefdom. In the early years, employees were paid in script redeemable only at the company store. McMillan's iron- fisted employment practices were typical of the age of the Robber Baron. He was generous, though, in providing free health care to his employees. He was a good manager and the company was successful. The company soon operated its own narrow-gauge railroad and ships. In 1929, the company was worth over one million dollars, which would be worth many millions today.

McMillan also developed the Staveless Barrel Co. Lime was shipped in wooden barrels, which were expensive. When he heard of a new machine that carved barrel halves from logs at a considerable savings, he wanted the company to buy the machine, but the Board of Directors was reluctant to spend the money in the midst of the Panic of 1893. Knowing a good deal when he saw it, McMillan invested $200 and a personal note (personal loan) to buy the machine and build a barrel factory. He sold the first order of barrels to the lime company for enough money to pay the note. He then had the lime company pay him $200 for negotiating the contract, offsetting his $200 cash investment. As a result, he acquired a valuable factory which cost him nothing but his imagination and a little effort. The factory produced 5,000 barrels a day, many of which were sold to the producers of coffee, candy, oatmeal, and fire clay. The minority shareholders sued him for defrauding the lime company, but the court found him innocent, and commended his good judgment. The factory was burned by an arsonist in 1920 and was not rebuilt.

McMillan served for many years as the Chairman of the San Juan County Republican Party and represented the area in the State Legislature. Republican candidates for county offices were personally selected by McMillan. He served on the State Railway Commission, which was created to establish equitable freight rates for ships and trains. He was accused of using his position to establish a preferential rate for the lime company. He denied the charge, but resigned from the commission and returned his salary. He was not charged with malfeasance.

Beginning in 1888, McMillan attended every state and national Republican convention, where he became friends with Teddy Roosevelt and other influential party leaders. Republicans who visited Roche Harbor were entertained lavishly. His visitors included ex-Presidents Theodore Roosevelt and William H. Taft. When Roosevelt and the progressive Republicans formed the Bullmoose Party in 1912, McMillan remained with the GOP. Although McMillan achieved most of his political goals, he did not achieve his goal of becoming a US Senator.

McMillan died on November 4, 1936, at the age of 81. At the time of his death, the company's fortunes were declining. There are several explanations for the decline. Local legends and many published accounts say the lime beds were exhausted, due to wasteful mining practices. When more efficient procedures became available, McMillan retained the older, wasteful practices. During this period, as McMillan got older, he lost interest in managing the firm and assigned the day-to-day administration to his youngest son, Paul. After McMillan died in 1936, Paul McMillan managed the company.

41

Neil Tarte, the President of Roche Harbor Co., insists large, workable lime deposits remain on the property. He says the lime company failed due to a shortage of fuel and to poor management. Limestone must be processed at high heat, and the only fuel on the island that creates enough heat is fir. A shortage of fir forced the company to reduce its operations. Tarte was the last manager of the Roche Harbor lime works. Etta Egeland, the dean of island historians, says the plant declined due to the lack of old-growth fir, which burns with the intense heat required to process lime.

Tarte's view of the poor management of the company under Paul McMillan is shared by many observers. Paul McMillan was not interested in managing the company. After the death of his older brother, Fred, his father asked him to manage the company. He reluctantly quit his job as an automobile salesman and returned to Roche Harbor. He was probably unsuited for such a stressful position as he was hospitalized repeatedly for psychiatric treatment. Those who knew him comment that he had serious emotional problems.

In 1956, the lime company was in financial difficulty when Mr. & Mrs. Ruben J. Tarte purchased the land, buildings, and business. Tarte founded Transport Storage and Distributing, Inc. in Seattle, in 1931. The company handled the storage and distribution of new automobiles in the Puget Sound area. In 1953, he invented the piggyback car used to haul automobiles. He also operated a Union Oil dealership in Seattle. He came from a seafaring family and visualized the property as a destination resort for yacht owners. After buying the property, the Tarte family lived on their yacht for several months and began cleaning the buildings and grounds and preparing them for a resort. They continued to produce lime to satisfy some remaining contracts, but production ended in 1957 when key equipment failed and could not be repaired economically. During the first year of operation under the Tartes, the docks were extended to moor yachts and the McMillan home was converted to a restaurant. The hotel was reopened three years later. Ruben Tarte died in 1968 and his youngest son, Neil, succeeded him as the president of the firm.

Tragedy struck the Tarte family on July 4, 1971. Robert Tangney, a member of the family, was working on a fireworks exhibit in the harbor when one of the fireworks exploded. Roy Franklin, a pioneer pilot, stood by to evacuate him to a hospital, but a severe rainstorm made it unsafe to fly. When the storm abated, Tangney was flown to a hospital. He died in route from a ruptured spleen caused by the concussion of the explosion. Independence Day fireworks were not resumed for many years.

CHAPTER FIVE:

SELF-GUIDED TOURS

This chapter contains of seven self-guided tours of the island. The first two tours combine stunning vistas with key aspects of the island's political and natural history. The third tour is a walking tour of historic Friday Harbor. Tours four and five are quick tours to places of interest near Friday Harbor. Tour six is a guide to the nature trail at American Camp. Tour seven is a guide to stunning nighttime sights from the bluff at the American Camp National Historic Park.

TOUR ONE : CATTLE POINT, AMERICAN CAMP, JAKLE'S FARM, AND TWO HISTORIC CHURCHES

Distance: 20.1 miles. A map follows page 5.

Time: Three hours, or longer, by automobile

Six hours, or longer, by bicycle

Services: Several picnic sites are included on the tour; some provide drinking water and restrooms. Food, beverages, and fuel are not available after leaving Friday Harbor.

44

Bicycles: This tour is well suited to bicycles. A .33 mile section of the road has a steep grade which forces many riders to dismount. With that exception, the tour is well suited for bicycling. A 1.3 mile section of the road is graveled, but an alternate, paved route is available. Restrooms and drinking water are available at the half-way mark. The roads do not have paved shoulders, so keep to the right side of the pavement to leave room for cars, trucks, and campers. Bicycle riders are subject to the traffic rules for automobiles.

Start on Spring Street in downtown Friday Harbor. Go up the hill to the Y intersection of Spring and Argyle Sts. and turn left on Argyle St. Argyle St. was built by volunteer labor in the winter of 1889/90 as the Argyle Wagon Rd. to connect the new community of Friday Harbor with the older community of Argyle. The first three blocks of this street have an interesting history. After the wagon road was completed, leading merchants began building homes along this street. A few of those homes were moved recently to make way for commercial buildings, but most of the others have been restored. The houses fall into two distinct groups. The ones built before 1900, tend to be smaller and are largely devoid of ornamentation. The post-1900 houses are larger and frequently display more ornamentation. THESE ARE PRIVATE RESIDENCES. THEY ARE NOT OPEN TO THE PUBLIC.

The first house on the left is the oldest house on this side of the block. It was built for Mr. & Mrs. G.B. Driggs. Driggs was a Friday Harbor merchant. He owned the entire block and grew several acres of strawberries. The fruit was sold locally and in Seattle. When Driggs experienced financial difficulties, he sold the property to Peter Lawsen, a farmer on the south end of the island. Mrs. Lawsen and two of their children lived here so the children could attend school in Friday Harbor. The Lawsens planted fruit trees on the property; the fruit was sold locally and shipped to Seattle. The land for the service station and the vacant lot to the left of the Driggs house were once occupied by four, small, one-story houses.

The next two houses on the left are honeymoon houses built by a prosperous merchant for two of his children. The one at 460 Argyle, is probably the newest house on the block. It was built about 1912 by L.B. Carter for his daughter Lettie. After her husband, George Nichols died, Lettie married William (Billy) Roark. Roark managed the dry goods department of his father-in-law's Blue Front Store and later operated Roark's Dry Goods Store.

The next house, at 470 Argyle, was built at the turn of the century by L.B. Carter for his son Alvie. Alvie worked in the grocery department of his father's Blue Front Store.

On the other side of the street, the house at 455 Argyle was built in about 1885 for Sheriff Newton Jones. It was later owned by Mr. & Mrs. Frank Dennison, and is now owned by Mrs. Dennison's niece. Dennison was a carpenter who previously served as the lighthouse keeper on Smith Island, in the Straits of Juan de Fuca

The house next to it, at 475 Argyle, was built for Mr. & Mrs. Peter A. Jensen. Jensen and G.B. Driggs operated a store at the corner of Spring and Second Sts., on the site of the present King's Market. Driggs and Jensen later operated separate stores.

The next house, at the corner of Argyle and Caines Sts., was built in 1898 for Mr. & Mrs. G.B. Driggs, who previously lived a block down the street. The house was restored by Mr. & Mrs. Ralph A. Rich.

The next house on this side of the street is perched high on the hill at the corner of Tucker and Caines Sts. It was built in 1905 by George Mullis, a carpenter and cabinet maker.

The house on the other side of the street, at 550 Argyle, was occupied by Mr. & Mrs. Isaac Sandwith. Mr. Sandwith was a county commissioner and a rural mail carrier. Mr. & Mrs. Sandwith operated the first jitney (taxi) service on the island.

Optional side trip: Those who like Victorian houses may want to take an optional side trip down Malcolm St. A lovely Victorian house stands a block down Malcom St. It was built in 1902 for Mr. & Mrs. Ross Tulloch. Mr. Tulloch was a descendant of a pioneer family on Orcas Island. Mrs. Tulloch, nee Mable Fogg, was from New England. Tulloch operated a hardware store at the corner of First and Spring Sts. The house displays a nice balance with a curved porch, arched windows, fancy shingles, and mixed-sized gables. This is not a particularly large or elaborate house, but it may be the finest Victorian house on the island. It is a private residence and is not open to the public. Turn around at the entrance to the storage buildings and return to Argyle St.

The house on Argyle next to Kingdom Hall was occupied for many years by Mr. & Mrs. William Fowle. Fowle operated the Progressive Variety Store in the post office building. He served briefly in the 1890's as the postmaster. The next two houses are of recent construction.

The house at 770 Argyle, was built in 1912 by John P. Paine, a local contractor. In 1914, he sold it to Mr. & Mrs. Cecil Carter. Mr. Carter was the president of the San Juan County Bank. It has been occupied for many years by Mr. & Mrs. Jack Fairweather.

The house on the other side of the street, at 755 Argyle, was built early in the twentieth century. It was the home of Mr. & Mrs. Robert Firth, Jr. It was recently restored by Larry and Roz Duthie. Firth's farm will be seen later at American Camp.

The two-story house at the corner of Argyle and Cedar Sts., was a farm home built for Mr. & Mrs. Peter Larsen, who homesteaded the property. Mr. Larsen operated a dairy and orchard. When the farm was subdivided, Cedar St. was placed through the center of the farm. Larsen's dairy barn stood on the site of the condominiums on the other side of Cedar St. The house was restored in the 1980's by Marilyn Francis.

At the County Fair Grounds, the white house with a Scout logo was the Elias F. Harpst residence, which stood behind Harpst's mortuary in downtown Friday Harbor. The house was donated to the Scouts when the downtown property was cleared for new buildings.

After Leaving Friday Harbor, watch for Griffin Bay. It is named for Charles J. Griffin, the first manager of the Hudson Bay Company's Bellevue Farm. The island in the bay is Dinner Island, which is occupied by three vacation homes. An unconfirmed account says it was named by Capt. G.H. Richards, of the Royal Navy, who stopped here for dinner.

After passing the airport, watch for a two-story, salmon-colored house on the right side of the road. It was built at the corner of Spring and Argyle Sts., where it was occupied by Mr. & Mrs. Frank Dennison, then by Mr. & Mrs. L.B. Carter. Mr. Carter was a prominent Friday Harbor merchant and property owner. The house was moved here to make way for the bank at the corner of Spring and Argyle Sts.

The next house on the right side of the road was occupied by Mr. & Mrs. J.O. Bergman, Jr. "Oscar" Bergman operated the Corner Store, which will be seen shortly.

The next intersection is Madden's Corner, named for Patrick and Daniel Madden, Irish immigrants who owned farms around the intersection. The first business on this corner was a blacksmith shop begun in 1877 by J. Dorley and operated later by his son, Ben. He was succeeded by Charlies Buchanan, then by Gunder Halvorsen, who moved the business to Friday Harbor. The shop stood behind the little house on the right side of Argyle St. This house replaced an older house that burned down. The blacksmith shop was in a barn behind the house which burned down in 1925.

On the other side of Argyle St. is the Corner Store, which was built in 1893, three years after the Argyle Wagon Rd. was completed. The store was built by the San Juan Trading Co., owned

48

by Norman E. Churchill and M.R. Noftsger. Churchill bought out Noftsger and later sold the building and business to J.O. Bergman, a German immigrant who operated a general store in Argyle. The store was operated for many years by J.O. Bergman, Jr., the son of J.O., and the son-in-law of Daniel Madden. The store closed in 1938 and Bergman died the following year. The store served briefly as a cabinet shop, but has been empty for several years.

The contractor's shop next to the Corner Store is the site of Woodman Hall, a lodge for the Industrial Workers of the World. The IWW was a socialist labor union known as the "Wobblies." The hall was built early in the century and was demolished in 1944. J.O. Bergman, who ran the Corner Store, looked after the hall.

The Argyle Wagon Rd. ended at this intersection where it joined Military Rd. Military Rd. began as a sixteen-mile trail through the woods connecting the US and British military camps. At first it was just wide enough for a horse and rider. It was widened later to accommodate wagons. It soon became the main island road. When the island roads were realigned early in this century, some parts of Military Rd. were abandoned; the remaining parts bear many names.

Turn left on Military Rd., which is now known as Cattle Point Rd. On your left, watch for The Meadows bed and breakfast which stands on the Daniel Madden homestead. The house was built in about 1892, but the first owner is unknown. The large trees in the yard are Garry Oaks. Several more can be seen in the next mile. They are numerous in this area, but uncommon on other parts of the island. Because of the trees, the hill on the right side of the road is called Oak Ridge.

Watch for Portland Fair Rd., about a mile away. In 1864, a one- room school was built on Portland Fair Hill to the right of Portland Fair Rd. It was a twenty by thirty foot log cabin built by volunteer labor for the island's first school district. It was called No. 1 School, from the name of the school district. For many years, it was the only public building on the island outside the military camps, so it was used for church services, lodge meetings, social gatherings, and political meetings. After a new school was built, the old school was converted to a barn. It was demolished in the 1960's.

The log school was replaced by a larger school on Cattle Point Rd., at the crest of Portland Fair Hill. The second schoolhouse was sold for $100 in 1942 and dismantled for the lumber. The site of the second school is now occupied by a modern house with attractive stone pillars at the entrance.

At Watson Rd., notice the farm in the distance, on the right side of Watson Rd. That was the Christopher Rosler farm. Rosler came to the island as a US soldier during the Pig War and remained after his enlistment expired in 1860. He died in 1907.

About a mile down the road, watch for a small sign identifying the Olympic Lights bed and breakfast. The house can be seen in the distance. It is a Victorian farmhouse built in 1895 by Andy Johnson to replace an earlier log house. Mrs. Johnson was a member of the pioneer Firth family. The Firth farm is seen later on this tour.

Turn right on the first road AFTER passing the entrance sign for the American Camp National Historic Park

Bicyclists: If you wish to avoid a 1.3 mile section of gravel road, remain on the paved road and turn right at Picketts Lane to return to the tour.

In 1850, the Hudson Bay Co. built a fishing station nearby, on Grandma's Cove. It consisted of a shed and vats for salting fish. The fish were caught by Indians, who exchanged sixty fish for one blanket. Two to three thousand barrels of fish were salted, packed, and shipped annually. Most went around the Horn to Europe.

In 1852, William Webster, a US citizen, built a trading post on this part of the island, but the exact location is unknown. The

Hudson Bay Co. claimed the island was British territory and objected to his presence, but Webster insisted the island was US territory and refused to move. As a result of this and other American encroachments, James Douglas, the Hudson Bay Co. manager, established a farm here in 1853 to strengthen the company's claim to the island. Douglas called it Belle Vue Farm, later Bellevue Farm, because of its stunning views of the Olympic Mountains. Charles J. Griffin, an Englishman, was the first farm manager. Most of the laborers were Kanakas, a name given to natives of Hawaii. They were excellent sailors and were eagerly recruited by English sea captains. Some Kanakas jumped ship and others were hired in Hawaii to work in the Pacific Northwest. The Hudson Bay Co. paid the Kanakas seven dollars a month, much less than they paid European workers. Bellevue Farm specialized in sheep raising, though some crops, pigs, and cattle were included. Log homes, bunkhouses, barns, and workshops were built on Bellevue Farm. Soon, flowers, vegetables, and fruit trees were planted near the buildings.

In 1858 and 1859, several unsuccessful Yankee gold miners came to the island to claim part of Bellevue Farm for themselves. One of them was Lyman Cutler, who built a cabin and began farming in the northwest corner of Bellevue Farm. Griffin complained that Cutler was trespassing and tried to get him to move but Cutler accused Griffin of trespassing on US territory. The conflict came to a head in 1859 when Cutler was awakened one morning to find a large black boar from Bellevue Farm rooting in his potato patch. Cutler had complained about that boar before--this time he shot it. The ensuing conflict led to the famous Pig War, which is described in Chapter 4.

On the left is the park interpretive center. This is the starting point for a walking tour of the US Army encampment and Bellevue Farm. The interpretive center stands near the site of the Randolph Rosler farm house. Rosler was a son of Christopher Rosler, whose farm was seen earlier on this tour. After the Army left the island, Rosler obtained this land and built a house for his family. The fruit trees at the beginning of the tour grew on the Bellevue Farm. An Army hospital stood on the property which Rossler converted to a barn. The barn was subsequently enlarged by adding lean-to sheds on all four sides. The hospital/barn stood near the trail, on the other side of the fruit trees. It burned down during the 1960's, probably from arson.

A flagpole and two old military buildings stand east of the interpretive center. The flagpole on the southeast corner of the parade ground was erected by the National Park Service on the site of the original Army flagpole. The large building was an officer's house. It was built partially of logs and partly of finished lumber. After the Army left, it was occupied by Mr. & Mrs. Robert Firth. In 1862, Firth replaced Charles Griffin as the manger of Bellevue Farm. Because of the conflict with the US and problems within the company, Hudson Bay Co. gave the farm to Firth by fee simple. In 1890, the widower Robert Firth retired and rented the farm to Robert, Jr. The younger Firth and his family later lived in Friday Harbor. Their home was seen on Argyle St.

The small building across the road was a laundress' house built of finished lumber brought from Ft. Bellingham. During the first month of the military occupation, Capt. George E. Pickett sent soldiers to Bellingham Bay to dismantle some new military buildings and erect them here. The portable buildings replaced the tents which first occupied the ridge. Additional buildings were built after the two countries agreed to a joint military occupation of the island. After the Army left in 1874, island residents bought or appropriated the buildings. Some were used here, but most of the twenty-eight primary buildings were moved to Friday Harbor, Argyle, and other places on the island.

The area is marked with numerous rock piles. The ones around the parade ground were probably begun by the soldiers. The farmers who occupied this ground enlarged the piles and started new rock piles. The ground is covered with a variety of grasses. When the land was acquired by the National Park Service, the native and introduced specie were allowed to take over the land.

1. Army officer's house, later used by the Firth family.

2. The Valley Church.

The redoubt (earthen fortifications) were built in the summer of 1859, in anticipation that the British would storm the encampment. A small Army cemetery is in the field below the fortifications. At one time, it had either fourteen or eighteen graves. All but two of the bodies were moved to a military cemetery at Port Townsend. The two remaining graves are unmarked. During the military occupation, the Army built a picket fence around the cemetery with an arch over the entrance. They have disappeared and the cemetery is difficult to find.

The site of the Bellevue Farm buildings are marked by a large flagpole. When the US Army arrived, the farm had seven small, one-story, log buildings. Those buildings and their foundations have all disappeared. The apple trees planted near the buildings produced fruit until early in this century; they have also disappeared. The Union Jack is flown here during the summer.

* * * * *

This area represents a unique climatalogical environment. The Olympic Mountains to the south create a "rain shadow" in this area. As moisture-laden clouds move in from the ocean they are compressed as they pass over the mountains. This causes moisture particles to form and fall as rain or snow. Some places in the Olympic Mountains receive over two hundred inches of rain per year. Having released their moisture in the mountains, the clouds tend to retain moisture as they leave the mountains. The driest area in the Olympic rain shadow is near Smith Island, in the middle of the Straits of Juan de Fuca.. The town of Sequim, directly across the sound, receives fifteen inches of precipitation per year, while this area receives nineteen inches per year. The low rainfall in this area clearly affects the environment, as Prickly-pear Cactus grow naturally on south-facing slopes. Before the National Park Service bought this land, the farmers grew spring wheat here, similar to the wheat grown in the dry areas of eastern Washington.

This area is the home of many birds and animals, including many deer and rabbits. The rabbits are classified as escaped domestic animals. At one time, thousands of them lived here but they nearly disappeared early in the 1980's. It is unknown whether they died from a disease or from another cause. In recent years they have begun multiplying. This area is also the home of the Columbia Black-tail Deer, a native species. They are reclusive, but the patient observer can find them here, and in many other parts of the island.

This grassy area is the home of the only Eurasian Skylarks known to live in the US. The birds were introduced in 1903 on the Saanich Peninsula, north of Victoria, and a few of them migrated here. They travel as far east as Iceberg Point on Lopez Island, but do not nest there. They have not migrated further because they require a dry, grassy environment and the damp, forested areas to the north, east, and south are inhospitable to them.

This area also is the home of several pair of Bald Eagles. The tall trees provide nesting sites near abundant food sources. Eagles prefer fish, which are abundant here, but they also eat carrion and small animals. At one time, this area was overrun with rabbits, which supplied a steady source of food. The eagles grow white head and tail feathers when they are four or five years old and sexually mature. Some live here permanently while others winter here. One pair of Golden Eagles are year-round residents. They usually eat small animals.

Several varieties of hawks live here, including Sharp-shinned Hawks, Red-tailed Hawks, and Rough-legged Hawks. Rough-legged Hawks winter here, while the others are year-round residents. They eat live animals and carrion and they frequently perch on branches, utility poles, and fences watching for food. This area is also the home for a few Turkey Vultures. They have a six foot wingspan, making them one of the largest birds in North America. A few vultures remain here throughout the year, but most winter in California. They only eat carrion.

* * * * *

Continue down the gravel road. At the stop sign, turn right on Picketts Lane. South Beach is at the end of the lane where restrooms, picnic tables, and firepits are available. This is one of the finest sandy beaches on the island. The currents add more sand each year. The currents also deposit driftwood. The name South Beach was assigned by the National Park Service to the dismay of island residents who called it Salmon Bank Beach. It is also known as Firewood Beach because some residents gather firewood here in the fall. Driftwood may be gathered at any time, but the Park Service prohibits operating chainsaws during the summer and in periods of high fire risk. Information about the wood-cutting season is available from the National Park Service office in Friday Harbor.

The adjoining water is part of the Straits of Juan de Fuca, which separate San Juan Island from the Olympic Peninsula. The straits are heavily traveled by ships entering and leaving Puget Sound. The ships in the distance may be tankers carrying Alaskan crude oil to refineries at Anacortes, or non-Alaskan crude to Canadian refineries. Other ships carry grain, logs, lumber, automobiles, and other heavy or bulky products. Occasionally, an aircraft carrier, cruiser, or other naval ship is seen traveling between the ocean and the Bremerton Naval Yard. Submarines from the Trident Base on the Hood Canal also pass through the straits. US submarines travel on the surface in these waters. Submerged Soviet submarines have been detected in this area. To your left, tug boats and barges can be seen traveling between Puget Sound and British Columbia and Alaska.

The waters in the left foreground cover a shallow, underwater ridge called Salmon Bank. The ridge is perpendicular to the shore and extends 1.75 miles into the straits. It is a hazard to ships. The Indians discovered that salmon swam close to the surface here, making it an excellent place to net fish. Archaeological research indicates an Indian summer village stood here for 2,700 years. The village was occupied during the summers when the Indians caught and preserved fish. A few Indians still lived here in the 1870's. Today, commercial and sport fishermen make large catches in this area. Frequently, a few boats are seen fishing while the others wait to place their nets in the best location.

The snow-capped Olympic Mountains may be seen across the straits. The plumes of smoke are from sawmills and paper plants on the Olympic Peninsula. In the distance, on the right, is Vancouver Island, in British Columbia. Victoria and its western suburbs can be seen on the southern tip of the island. The Straits of Juan de Fuca are to the left of Victoria.

FISHING BOATS

The fishing boats most frequently seen here are gillneters and purse seiners. The smaller boats are gillneters, which are usually operated by one person. One end of the 1,800-foot-long net is secured to a reel on the boat and the other end is attached to a buoy. The boat moves slowly away till the net is fully deployed. One edge of the net is equipped with floats to hold it near the surface; the other edge of the net is weighted with lead sinkers to keep it fully deployed. The edges of the net are called the cork line and the lead line. The net and boat drift in the current for about two hours while salmon are entangled in the net. The net is slowly retrieved and the fish are removed and stored for sale. Gillnetters usually work at night when their nets are less visible to the fish. They are frequently seen leaving the Friday Harbor marina shortly before sunset to get in position for the night's work.

The larger fishing boats seen in the area are usually purse seiners. They are operated by a crew of four or five. The net is usually mounted on a large reel on the after deck of the boat. One end of the net is secured to a large motor skiff which helps hold the net in position. After standing in the water for about two hours, the net is pulled into a circle to form the "purse". The net is then lifted into the boat. Purse seiners normally fish from sunrise to sunset. When the crew is not fishing, the broad-beamed, aluminum skiff is frequently winched onto the afterdeck.

Trollers fish off the coast, but are frequently seen in the area. They are a little smaller than a purse seiners and do not have a net reel or motor skiff. A long metal pole is mounted on each side of the boat. Four to eight baited fishing lines are attached to the poles. Trollers move slowly through the water to make the baited hooks look like a live fish. Trollers usually have a crew of two, the captain and "fish puller," who handles the lines. They are frequently at sea for up to a week. When the boats are not fishing, the long poles are folded in an upright position.

The largest boats are tenders, commonly called "fish buyers" or "buyer boats." They meet fishing boats at the fishing areas to purchase the catch. The tenders store fish in refrigerated holds till they are delivered to a processing plant. Many tenders display a sign indicating that the captain pays cash for fish.

To continue the tour, return to the highway. Turn right at the stop sign, then make a left turn into the Jakle's Lagoon parking area. The area between the bottom of this hill and Griffin Bay is the site of San Juan Town, the first town on the island. It began as a tent town in July, 1859 to supply liquor and prostitutes to soldiers. Military commanders tried to control alcohol sales and prostitution, but with little success. Although it began as a tent town, twenty small wooden buildings were soon built for a bakery, a butcher shop, and various disorderly houses. Contemporary accounts describe them as dirty little shacks. When the Army left in 1874, Waterman & Katz, of Port Townsend, opened a general store in San Juan Town, in an old military warehouse. The store sold flour, sugar, coffee, salt, cloth, guns, ammunition, tobacco, tools, lanterns, tobacco, liquor, farm implements, and other items required by the settlers. The proprietor, Israel Katz, was a genial man who was well liked. Like most storekeepers, he operated a bar in the back of the store. From 1874 until about 1880, it was the largest and most popular store on the island. When the Army left, the other businesses closed or moved to Argyle.

The Katz Store and the rest of San Juan Town were destroyed on July 4, 1890, while most people were at an Independence Day picnic at Union Grove Hall in the San Juan Valley. "Whispering" Pete Seary, the Katz farm caretaker, was burning dry grass when the fire escaped and spread to the town. The loose-stone foundations of the buildings could be seen for many years, but they have since disappeared.

The wooded area on the opposite side of the parking lot is the site of Jakle's Farm. During the 1860's, Frank Bryant, a US soldier, built a log cabin here for himself, his wife Eliza, and their baby. Eliza was probably the second white woman to live on the island. Frank drowned while hunting ducks and Eliza married George Jakle, another soldier. At the end of his enlistment, Jakle remained on the farm. Neither the Bryants nor the Jakles had a legal claim to the land. Like most settlers, they "squatted" on the land, hoping to secure a legal claim after the boundary dispute was resolved. The Jakles could not secure a claim because the Army held the land as a military reservation. The claim was established in 1860 by Capt. Lewis Cass Hunt, the camp commandant, who expanded the military reservation to the entire peninsula in an effort to control liquor sales. Since they could not claim to the land, the Jakles leased the farm until 1927, when the Army relinquished its claim to the eighty- seven-year-old widow. The Jakle family owned the land until it was acquired by the National Park Service. In 1870 the farm included a four-room house, a barn, a woodshed, a wagon shed, a dairy, a root cellar, and a chicken house. Twenty-five acres were under cultivation, with additional land used for pasture. Later, Jakle built a larger, two-story house. The house burned down in 1936 and was not rebuilt. The remaining buildings were demolished by the National Park Service.

This parking lot is the starting place for the Jakle's Lagoon nature trail. Numbered stakes have been placed along the path by the San Juan Horticultural Society which correspond to the plant descriptions in Tour 6. The site of Jakle's farm buildings is identified in the tour. The lagoons in this area are an excellent place to observe seals, shore birds, and water birds.

To continue Tour 1, return to the paved road and turn left.

On the right is the West Sen. Jackson overlook. This promontory provides a splendid overview of the Straits of Juan de Fuca, the Olympic Peninsula, and Vancouver Island.

A little further is the East Sen. Jackson overlook. The view from this promontory is similar to the view from the previous overlook. Cattle Point Lighthouse is visible from the east overlook. The hill on the north side of the road is Mt. Finlayson, a 292 foot high gravel moraine--a gravel pile deposited during the last ice age. A trail leads to the top of the hill, which provides an excellent view.

The Sen. Jackson overlooks are excellent places to observe ships and lighthouses at night. A nocturnal tour of these sights is given in Tour 7.

A little further down the road is a small vehicle turnout for Cattle Point Lighthouse. A short trail leads from the parking lot to the lighthouse. If the parking lot is full, additional parking is available one tenth of a mile down the road. The first lighthouse was built here in the nineteenth century; the present lighthouse was built in 1935..

When walking to the lighthouse, please remain on the trail. This area once supported a large population of rabbits. Most of them are gone, but hundreds of rabbit holes remain. Stepping in a hidden rabbit hole can cause a nasty fall.

After leaving the lighthouse, drive to the parking lot at the Cattle Point Interpretive Area/Coast Guard Wireless Station. Interpretive signs are posted around the shelter and a splendid viewpoint is available near the bluff.

Facilities: Water, restrooms, picnic tables, a shelter, and a stove. If it is too windy to enjoy a picnic here, save your lunch for the next stop on the tour. **This is the last drinking water source on the tour.**

Cattle Point probably received its name on Dec. 13, 1853, when the Hudson Bay Co. unloaded 1,300 sheep and a few cattle near this point. The animals were destined for Bellevue Farm. The Coast Guard Wireless Station was built in the 1920's to house a direction-finding radio antenna. When mariners could not establish their location from visual cues, direction-finding antennas could pinpoint a ship's location by triangulating on a ship's radio transmissions. The ship's location was then transmitted to the ship so it would not go aground. Shore-based direction finding stations were replaced by shipboard direction finders, and later by radar. The Wireless Station was closed on Nov. 15, 1930. The property was eventually transferred to the Washington Department of Natural Resources as a wildlife refuge and interpretive center.

Lopez Island is about one hundred yards east of Cattle Point and Goose Island is in the left foreground. When the state proposed building a bridge between Lopez and San Juan Islands, a local developer bought Goose Island hoping it would be needed for a bridge pier. When the bridge plan failed, he sold the island to the Nature Conservancy for the amount he paid for it. The island is administered by the University of Washington Marine Laboratory as a protected breeding site for Glaucous-winged Gulls, Oystercatchers, and Harbor Seals.

The nearest part of Lopez Island is Davis Point. The sheltered bay to the right of the point is Davis Bay. They are probably named for James L. and Amelia Davis, who arrived on Lopez Island in 1869 and operated a farm near the point. Mrs. Davis may have been the first white woman to live on Lopez Island. The small island just off Davis Point is Deadman Island. The origin of that name is unknown. The snow-capped mountain in the distance is Mt. Baker, a volcano in the Cascade Mountains.

The water between Cattle Point and Davis Point is Cattle Pass, the southern entrance to Middle Channel. Rising and falling tides cause substantial tide rips through Cattle Pass. Small boats have difficulty moving against the tide, so some sailors, especially the commercial fishermen, use a counter current running between Cattle Point and Goose Island. Navigating the shallow, narrow channel requires a thorough knowledge of hidden rocks and tricky currents--plus skillful seamanship.

An additional ten miles remain on this tour. When leaving the parking lot, turn left and travel toward Friday Harbor. After passing the intersection of Picketts Lane, watch for a small sign identifying the American Camp Picnic Ground. Turn right at the roadside marker, then turn right again to enter the parking lot. This picnic ground is popular with local residents who usually call it Fourth of July Beach. The name arose because Independence Day celebrations were held here for many years. It does not have restrooms or water fountains, but its natural beauty offsets the lack of amenities. When the prevailing winds blow from the west or south, the beach is sheltered from the wind. The picnic area is visible from the parking lot. To reach the beach, go to the picnic area, turn left and follow the path to the beach.

The beach faces Griffin Bay, which was named for Charles J. Griffin, the first manager of Bellevue Farm. The landmass at the north end of the bay is Pear Point. The gravel pit and the southern edge of Friday Harbor are visible on the point. The large yellow building to the left of the gravel pit is the fish cannery at Jackson Beach. The south end of Shaw Island is to the right of Pear Point. Further to the right is Turtle Mountain on Orcas Island.

To continue the tour, return to the highway and turn right. There are disputes about the place where Lyman Cutler shot the boar, but the best accounts suggest the site is about one mile down this road. Watch for the Homestead Trailer Park on the left side

61

of the road, then continue until reaching a large barn on the left side of the road. Cutler's cabin and potato patch were probably in the field on the east side of the highway (the side opposite the barn). This area has been farmed for over a century and no evidence of his cabin or potato patch remains. The site is on private property--do not trespass.

At Madden's Corner, turn left onto Madden Lane. (The name of the road was changed in 1987 and many maps still identify it as Cemetery Rd.) This was part of the old Military Rd. Drive slowly, a beautiful view will appear suddenly on the left.

The Valley Church, formerly Immanuel Presbyterian Church, is the oldest church in the county. The cornerstone was laid in August, 1878, the building as completed in 1882. Construction money was raised by private donations, including a $400 grant by the Seattle Presbyterian Presbytery and $150 raised at an 1874 church festival. The land for the church and the old part of the cemetery was donated by Matthias Lundblad, a Norwegian immigrant. Lundblad purchased and planted many of the trees.

Much of the credit for building the church goes to the Rev. Thomas J. Weeks, who came to the island in 1870, after receiving his Licentiate. He was ordained in 1872, two years after arriving on the island. During his early years on the island, he did not receive a salary, but depended on the collection plate for his livelihood. The plate was passed once a month and he was fortunate to receive a few coins. This was supplemented by donations received during his annual pastoral calls, which netted about twenty-five dollars a year. In the early years, Weeks was so poor he was unable to buy new clothing and lived in the homes of charitable parishioners. At one home, his room was a corner of the attic. When the US Army left the island in 1874, he and his bride moved to the Captain's house at American Camp. From 1884 to 1890, he supplemented his income as the part-time postmaster at San Juan Town. Postmasters did not receive a salary, but were paid a percentage of the stamps they canceled. Since few letters were sent from this post office, his income from "cancellations" was minimal.

He also earned a little money maintaining the lighthouse at Cattle Point. Weeks also went to Lopez Island every two weeks to conduct a service in the schoolhouse. The Rev. & Mrs. Weeks left the island in April of 1891 so their children could attend high school.

When the Rev. Weeks arrived on the island he wrote to his friends that many island families consisted of a White man and an Indian women who were living together without the benefit of marriage. He also complained about drinking and gambling by many island residents. In time, he persuaded many couples to get married and to reform their lives. Many old island families have strong ties to this little church.

After the Rev. Weeks left, the parish was without a pastor for over a year. His successor, the Rev. J.M.C. Warren, discovered only two members remained in the church, but he soon increased the membership to fourteen. In 1894, some of the Presbyterians formed a new congregation in Friday Harbor and built a new church there in 1897. Membership in the country church dwindled and the remaining members eventually transferred to the Friday Harbor congregation.

By 1947, the country church was badly deteriorated and there was talk of demolishing it, but Ella Dightman led the effort to restore it. In 1951, the church and cemetery were deeded to San Juan County Cemetery Dist. 1. The church was renamed the Community Church and was used by several new congregations until they could obtain their own church. The kerosene lamps in the church were replaced with electric lights in the 1950's, when the church was used by the Episcopalian congregation. The Episcopalians said a little mouse lived in the organ. They say he sat quietly during the services and stroked his whiskers. The church has not been used for several years.

The first church on the island was St. Francis Roman Catholic Church, which stood across the road. The parishioners built a small log church 1860, on land donated by Daniel Madden. The church was in the present St. Francis Cemetery, on the right side of the cemetery lane. The church burned down in 1874, the year the Presbyterian Church was completed. If the log church was still standing and in use, it would be the oldest Roman Catholic Church in Western Washington. The first recorded burial in the cemetery was in 1872, but several unrecorded and unmarked graves were visible at that time. Older residents say there are many unmarked and undocumented graves in this cemetery.

After the first church burned, the parishioners erected a temporary church on the site of the first church. The temporary church was replaced by a larger framed church erected across the lane, in the present grassy field. The construction date for the third church is unknown, but it may have been in the 1880's. The third church was moved to Friday Harbor in 1959, where it is seen at the end of this tour. The old church outhouse still stands among the trees.

The lane through St. Francis Cemetery was part of Military Rd. The county realigned the roads in this area in 1906, and this section stopped being used. Several graves are now in the Military Rd. right of way. The cemetery is primarily maintained by volunteer labor. One Saturday morning each spring and fall, many parishioners gather to cut the weeds, mow the grass, trim the trees, and remove litter. The work is followed by a picnic lunch. Lunch is followed by a dads-and-kids softball game, with some dads and some kids on each side. The game is played under special rules; the dads and older kids play competitively, but the little kids are never struck out or put out.

When leaving the cemetery, turn right. At the end of Madden Lane, turn right on Douglas Rd. At the end of Douglas Rd., turn right on San Juan Valley Rd.

Observe The Speed Limit As You Enter The Town.

In town, San Juan Valley Rd. becomes Spring St. Stay on Spring St. and turn left on Price St. Enter the parking lot next to St. Francis Roman Catholic Church. This is the church that was moved to town in 1959. When the church stood in the cemetery, it had a steeple, but no bell. The steeple was removed when the church was moved and it was not rebuilt. The large cross on the front of the church was added after the building was moved. Visitors are welcome to enter the church.

The furnishings in the nave are probably as old as the church. When the church was in the country, it was heated by a pot-belly stove which stood in front of the present pulpit. When the church was moved to town, the stove was replaced by central heating. The stove space was then used for additional pews, which were built to match the original pews. The stations of the cross (the pictures on the walls) are inexpensive prints. Their age is unknown, but they have been there as long as anyone can remember.

The sanctuary has been remodeled three times. It was remodeled the first time in 1958, shortly before the church was moved to town. At that time, the original furnishings were replaced with elaborate furnishings from Germany. The imported furnishings were replaced in the 1970's with temporary furnishings designed to conform to the revised liturgy. The temporary furnishings were replaced in about 1981 with locally-produced furnishings made of mahogany. The cross above the altar is made of mahogany. The corpus and inscription attached to it are carved from olive wood.

The two-story house next to the church parking lot is a museum operated by the San Juan Historical Society. The house was built in 1890 by James F. King to replace a log cabin that burned down. The house stood on a 445 acre dairy and fruit farm which encompassed much of present Friday Harbor. King homesteaded here in 1877 and later purchased additional land. He also operated a butcher shop and freight business. George E. Peacock bought King's house in 1966 and donated it to the historical society for a museum.

Several historic buildings stand behind the museum. The stone and wood building is an original farm building. The stone portion of the building was used to store milk, fruit, and vegetables; it may be the oldest building on the site. The small building with the barred windows is the old county jail, which stood near the courthouse.

The log cabin was built near Mitchell Bay in 1891 by James and Edward Scribner. When it was finished, Edward send for his wife and three small children; they lived in the cabin till 1909, when they moved to Friday Harbor. Mr. Scribner and his sons were commercial fishermen and they continued to use the cabin as a fishing camp. For many years, Scribner's boat, *Medea,* was chartered by the University of Washington Marine Laboratory. The boat was named for one of his daughters. The Scribner cabin was donated to the museum in 1988. The large storage building at the rear of the lot was built in the 1980's to house old farm equipment used on island farms.

This is the end of the tour. To return to the starting point, turn right when you leave the parking lot. At the stop sign, turn left and travel two blocks.

TOUR TWO: ENGLISH CAMP, ROCHE HARBOR

WHALE WATCH PARK, PLUS STUNNING

MARINE VISTAS.

Distance: 33.7 miles. A map follows page 5.

Time: A half a day by automobile. All day by bicycle.

Services: A full-service restaurant is available during the tourist season at Roche Harbor, one-third of the way through the tour. (Lunch, including beverage and tip, begins at about $12. Dinner begins at about $18.) Picnic sites, with water and restrooms, are available on the tour. Snacks, cold beverages, and gasoline may be purchased at the Roche Harbor Store.

Bicycles: This tour is popular with experienced bike riders, but parts of it are unsuited for weak or novice riders. Weak or novice riders may enjoy the trip to Roche Harbor and English Camp, which passes through rolling hills, but they should return to Friday Harbor via Roche Harbor Rd. or West Valley Rd. to avoid the difficult middle section of the tour. (The two routes are about the same length, but West Valley Rd. has steeper grades.) Restrooms and drinking water are available at several points on the trip, but not in the first ten miles or in the last eleven miles of the tour. Overnight camping is available at Lakedale Campground, near the start of the tour, and the San Juan County Park, near the middle of the tour. (Campground information appears on page 17) The middle third of the tour includes several long, steep grades which force many riders to dismount. A two-mile section of road in the middle third is graveled and no alternate route is available. The roads are narrow and do not have paved shoulders. Stay in single file on the right side of the pave-

67

ment to leave room for cars, trucks, and campers. Bicycle riders
are subject to the traffic rules for automobiles.

From the Royal Theatre on Spring St., go up Second St. to
the crest of the hill. The little white church at the crest of the hill
was built in 1900 as a Seventh-Day Adventist Church. The congregation met infrequently, so the twenty-two by thirty foot building was rented to the school district to relieve a classroom
shortage. (The school was between the new theater and the courthouse.) For several years, the first, second, and third grades were
taught simultaneously in this one-room school. A new school was
built in 1914 and the church stood empty. It was purchased by the
Christian Science Society, in 1923. The society paid $350 for the
building, with $250 down and $5 monthly payments to cover the
balance. The Sunday school wing was added in 1970. The front
porch was replaced by a foyer in 1973.

Go down the hill on Guard St., then turn right on Tucker Ave.
At the bottom of the hill, park on the side of the road to look at a
neighborhood with an interesting history. The area on the right
side of the road once served as an Indian campground. Most Indians lived in tents but some built shanties and grew gardens here.
They frequently earned money by catching salmon and selling
them at the canneries. Some went from door-to-door selling fresh
salmon and clams.

In 1894, A.C. Brown built a sawmill near the water, the bottom of the present Harbor St. Brown was a Seventh-Day Adventist who helped build the little white church, seen earlier. He cus-
tomarily blew mill's steam whistle at 12 o'clock sharp-- except on
Saturday when he went to church. Having observed the sabbath
the previous day, Brown ran the sawmill on Sundays. His good
friend and neighbor, the Rev. T.L. Dyer, was the Methodist Minister. The Methodist Church was a few blocks away and Brown
took great delight in disrupting Dyer's Sunday service with a
prolonged blast of the noon whistle. Dyer gave up trying to preach
over the noise, so he dismissed the congregation as soon as Brown

blew the noon whistle. They remained good friends. The mill burned down in about 1910 and was not rebuilt.

This area was once known as McDonald's Beach, where young people gathered for swimming and picnics. The beach was named for a Mr. McDonald who operated some hop-drying houses here. When the area was platted for residential development, it was named Friday Harbor Playground. When some of the homes were built here, contractors unearthed huge sawdust deposits from Brown's sawmill.

The large, brown, two-story house on the left side of Tucker Ave. was built near the turn of the century by Joe and Ben Groll, who were part owners of a fish cannery. Mr. & Mrs. Joe Groll lived in the house until they sold it in 1920 to Mr. & Mrs. Warren Dightman. Mr. Dightman operated a livery stable and Mrs. Dightman was a midwife. She attended home births throughout the island and brought women to her home for childbirth. Later, she used the house as a nursing home.

The Groll-Dightman house originally stood on a forty acre plot, which has since been subdivided. Many of the houses in this subdivision were moved here. Some came from the island, but others came from Seattle-Tacoma International Airport. The houses were transported from Seattle on barges and unloaded at the waterfront on your right.

The one-story, yellow house at 465 Tucker Ave. also was built near the turn of the century by Joe and Ben Groll. It was occupied by Mr. & Mrs. Ben Groll and is now owned by a descendant

CAUTION: The first three miles of Roche Harbor Rd. are heavily patrolled by the sheriff's deputies. Many visitors receive traffic tickets for exceeding the speed limit in this area.

Large blackberry bushes grow along the roadsides throughout the island. Early settlers planted blackberries; the birds ate the berries and spread the seeds throughout the island. The berries are bitter until they turn dark black, when they become very sweet. You may pick blackberries along the roadside, but do not enter private property to pick them.

After leaving town, watch for a flock of turkeys that lives in this area. They were introduced many years ago as game birds, but are rarely hunted. The birds are rather tame and are sometimes seen feeding near homes. During the winter, the flock sometimes wanders into Friday Harbor to find food.

Sportsman's Lake is three miles from town on the left side of the road. It is owned by the county. The property between the road and the lake is privately owned, but a public access lane is available. There are several natural lakes in this part of the island. Some, like this one, have been enhanced with small dams. This is an excellent place to catch Largemouth Bass. It is also an excellent place to see water birds, especially Mergansers. Other birds include Barrow's Goldeneyes, and Common Goldeneyes, Double-crested Cormorants, ospreys, and gulls. In the summer, swallows and swifts are seen skimming above the water feeding on insects. In the winter, Trumpeter Swans, an endangered species, are seen feeding here. They summer in Alaska and British Columbia.

After passing Egg Lake Rd. watch for Dream Lake on your left. This privately-owned lake was developed from a marsh as part of Lakedale Campground.

70

After Dream Lake, the road goes through 3.7 miles of second-growth forest. Upon leaving the forest watch for Westcott Bay on your left. From the farm gate nearest the forest, you can see the length of Westcott Bay. The entrance to the bay is formed by White Point on the right and Delacombe Point on the left. White point was the site of the first lime quarry on the island.

The Salish Indians noticed that many ducks flew through the narrow passes in this area. They strung nets made of vines across the passes, about ten feet above the water. Ducks flying low over the water at dusk or dawn could not see the nets and were trapped. The nets were lowered in the morning to retrieve the birds, most of whom were still alive. Most of the meat was dried and smoked for winter consumption. This area still supports a large population of water birds.

* * * * *

When entering Roche Harbor Resort, notice the small cottages near the entrance arch. They were built in the 1920's for married, caucasian workers. They are now rented by the week to visitors. The bright red building with the large windows was built in the 1920's as a one-room school. John S. McMillan, the president of the Roche Harbor Lime Co., was careful to control costs. Operating a school at company expense exempted the company from school taxes on over 4,000 acres and many buildings.

After passing the entrance arch, turn left and follow the paved road to the bottom of the hill. As you descend the hill, the old quarries can be seen on the left. DO NOT ENTER THE QUARRIES. THEY ARE HAZARDOUS DUE TO FALLING ROCKS. At the bottom of the hill, make a sharp right turn and park in the graveled parking area.

The rock and brick structures above the parking lot are the fire chambers of Kiln Battery Two, the new kilns built shortly after the turn of the century. A large steel cylinder, supported by a wooden crib, extended above each fire chamber. A narrow-gauge railroad ran above the top of the kilns to deliver crushed rock. The present road and parking lot occupy the site of a large processing building and warehouse. A loading dock extended into the water. The building burned down in 1923 and was rebuilt within a few months. In 1942, the railroad and some of the processing equipment were sold for scrap metal. The warehouse and processing building were demolished in 1971.

Walk toward the buildings and watch on your right for two Fairbanks-Morse generators. These diesel-fired generators supplied power to the homes and work places till the late 1950's, when when one of the generators failed and it was cheaper to use electricity from the local electric utility. The generators were housed in a metal building which has disappeared, except for the concrete floor.

Now go to the company store, to the left of the gas pumps. The deck on the side of the store offers an excellent overview of the property. The Hotel de Haro on your right began as a Hudson Bay Co. trading post. McMillan enlarged the building and converted it to a hotel in 1887. The McMillans lived in Tacoma, but when they visited Roche Harbor, they lived in the hotel. For many years, the employees' dining room was on the main floor of the hotel. The hotel also housed many guests, including ex- Presidents Teddy Roosevelt (who came twice) and William Howard Taft. The hotel closed in 1942 and was reopened in 1960, after extensive remodeling.

To the left of the hotel, near the water, is the McMillan home, which has been enlarged and converted to a restaurant. The home was created in 1924, by enlarging an existing house. The octagonal structure on the end of the building was added in recent years for a cocktail lounge. It mimics an octagonal pergola which stood there when the McMillans lived in the house.

On the hill, above the restaurant, is the home of Paul McMillan, the youngest son. It previously stood on the restaurant site,

3. J.S. McMillan's house, now used as a restaurant.

4. English Camp Parade Ground.

and was moved in about 1924 to facilitate enlarging the new McMillan home. It is now occupied by an employee.

The building with the cross on the roof is the chapel of Our Lady of Good Voyage, a Roman Catholic chapel. It was built in the nineteenth century as a one-room school, which was replaced in the 1920's by the red school near the resort entrance. After the red school was built, the McMillans converted the old school to a Methodist church. Services were conducted by a circuit-riding minister from Orcas Island. The Tarte family converted it to a Roman Catholic chapel. It is the only privately-owned Catholic chapel in the US. It is a popular place for weddings.

The workers' cottages and the red school are to the left of the chapel. Tennis courts and a swimming pool stand in front of the cottages. The large, metal object near the water, to the left of the tennis courts, is the boiler of the sixty-ton, tugboat, *Roche Harbor*. The boat was beached there in 1938 after fifty years of service and was burned by vandals in 1975. The wheel house of the *Roche Harbor* stands at the end of this dock and supports an array of flags.

In the foreground is the modern marina. During the McMillan years, a short ferry dock extended from the front of the garden for daily stops by the Black Ball Line, the predecessor to the Washington State Ferries. Ferry service was discontinued in about 1929, after Friday Harbor was added to the route.

From the end of the deck you can see a large, modern house on a point of land. It is the home of Neil and Margaret Tarte and stands on the site of the Staveless Barrel Co. The small island in front of the Tarte home is Pearl Island. The larger island to the left of Pearl is Henry Island. During the British occupation, Augustus "Guss" Hoffmeister raised cattle on Henry Island to supply meat to the Royal Marines. Keeping the cattle on an island eliminated the need for fences. Henry and Pearl Islands are not connected by a bridge, so residents and visitors leave their cars at Roche Harbor and commute in small boats.

This deck provides access to a clothing store, a laundromat, public restrooms, and a postal substation. The building is an old lime company warehouse. A post office was established near here in 1882, when the Scurr brothers operated the lime works.

The company store retains much of the appearance of an old country store. During the winter, a row of shelves are removed and replaced by a wood-burning stove and a lunch table. The country-store atmosphere is particularly noticeable in the winter when residents stand around the stove to warm their hands, read their mail, and meet their neighbors.

Now, walk toward the hotel. The two kilns nearest the real estate office are the oldest kilns on the site. They were here when McMillan bought the property. Some say they were built by the Royal Marines, though that cannot be proven. The other two kilns were added by McMillan in 1886, shortly after he bought the property. He identified these four kilns as Kiln Bank One.

If you look between the hotel and the real estate office, you will notice an ornate, unpainted, two-story house behind the hotel. This is the Doctor's House, which was built in about 1898 for Dr. Victor J. Capron, the company doctor. The house also may have been occupied by another company physician, a Dr. Harrison, who later practiced on Orcas Island. The Doctor's House has been unoccupied for many years

The brick sidewalk in front of the hotel is called the Yellow Brick Road. It is made of fire bricks reclaimed from Kiln Bank One. The garden was planted by Mrs. McMillan and was maintained for many years by Mrs. Ruben Tarte. It is a popular place for weddings.

The hotel has an interesting history. Part of the building is a log building built by the Hudson Bay Co. as a trading post. It was probably built during the joint military occupation of the island, when the Hudson Bay Co. shipped lime from this harbor. When the Scurr brothers owned the property, they used it as a bunkhouse. McMillan expanded the building and converted it to a hotel. He left the log building in place, but covered it with milled siding to match the rest of the building. In the 1890's it was advertised as one of the finest hotels north of San Francisco and boasted a Japanese chef "who knew all the recipes". The McMillans lived in the hotel when they visited Roche Harbor. It also housed customers, drummers (sales representatives), and other visitors. Its best-known guest was ex-president Teddy Roosevelt, who visited twice. When the McMillans entertained large groups, they used the lobby for a dining room. The upper floors of the hotel are reserved for registered guests, but visitors may examine the lobby, which is part of the original log building. Many interesting pictures, including a grand portrait of Pres. Roosevelt, are displayed there. Script for the company store is displayed in the corner opposite the hotel desk.

After examining the lobby, walk down the Yellow Brick Road and enter the grassy plaza on the right. McMillan designed this as a banquet court. The huge fireplace was used to prepare food for lawn parties. Old photographs show a large tent erected over the court, stretching from the hotel to the fireplace, with the sides open for ventilation. The building at the rear of the court is the Pavilion, a conference and dining room built on the upper level of the banquet court. It has a huge fireplace like the one on the lower court. Both fireplaces were built by McMillan; the building was built by Neil Tarte. From the banquet court, notice the row of French doors on the end of the hotel. The room behind the doors was built as a bandstand for the banquet court. The McMillans called it the Music Room, and it still goes by that name. It is now used as a bunkhouse for musicians.

The restaurant occupies the former John McMillan residence. It was build in four stages. The one-story portion at the entrance is the oldest part, which was built as an employee's house. The tall, ornate portion of the building was built in the 1920's, when the house was expanded to become the McMillan residence. The upper level of the restaurant dining room occupies the McMillan family living room, and dining room. The bar in the basement occupies McMillan's office. The tree in the center of the bar is part of the original construction. The octagonal cocktail lounge was added by the Tartes to replicate an octagonal pergola used by the McMillans. The Tartes also expanded the west side of the house to enlarge the dining room. The restaurant lobby features handsome woodwork and a beautiful pair of deSeures vases.

SUNSET FLAG CEREMONY: From Memorial Day to Labor Day, the resort conducts a flag ceremony that can be observed from throughout the grounds. The ceremony begins at sunset. The house flag, the Washington State flag, the Canadian flag, and the Union Jack are lowered slowly with the appropriate anthem. Then the Stars and Stripes are lowered to the sound of taps. The ceremony ends with a cannon shot. Service stops in the restaurant and hotel during this nine minute service and visitors are asked to remain quiet so that others may enjoy the ceremony.

The tour resumes as you leave the parking lot. As you turn the corner at the end of the parking lot, notice a green, metal maintenance building. Jap Town, the residence for oriental employees, stood just beyond the metal building. The oriental employees worked in the farm, garden, and house. The Japanese- American workers, regardless of their citizenship, were interned in 1942. When they were released from internment, they did not return to Roche Harbor. The small dwellings stood empty for many years and eventually collapsed.

Return to the resort entrance. Upon reaching the entrance arch, do not pass through the arch but continue straight ahead on a narrow road. At the intersection, take the road that curves to the left. Watch on the right for small white picket fences. These are part of the employees cemetery. Most of the graves are now unmarked because the wooden headstones have disappeared. A cemetery for oriental employees is higher on the hill, but no monuments remain.

A few hundred feet beyond the employees cemetery, a small sign points to the McMillan Mausoleum, which is a short walk up the trail. McMillan designed the limestone mausoleum near the end of his life. It is based on principals established by the Masonic Order and examples he saw in Europe. The table represents the family table with one chair for each member. The broken column represents the unfinished state of life upon death. The mausoleum was designed to include a bronze dome with a maltese cross on top. McMillan ordered the dome from a Virginia foundry shortly before his death, but his son canceled the order because they did not have enough money to pay for it. The chairs are crypts for the family members' ashes. The family is all interred here. Out of respect for the dead, please do not sit on the chairs.

Biographies of the McMillan children tell sad stories. John, the oldest son, died at birth. Fred, the second son, died at the age of 41. Dorothy died in 1980, at the age of 86; she lived in mental institutions during much of her adult life. Paul, the youngest son, was married twice and had two natural children and an adopted child. His wives and natural children are believed to be dead, but they are not buried here. Paul died at the age of 75. Throughout his adult life, he was deeply embittered by the abuse he received from his father, who openly favored his older brother, Fred. His adopted daughter, the heir to the McMillan estate, is still living.

*****

To continue the tour, return to the entrance arch. Travel 1.3 miles on Roche Harbor Rd., then turn right at West Valley Rd.

Bicyclists: The next water source is 8.1 miles from Roche Harbor.

Travel 1.3 miles on West Valley Rd., then turn right to enter English Camp historic park. Park in the parking lot and walk down the short trail to the historic site.

Facilities: The restrooms are at the upper end of the parking lot. Drinking water is not available here.

This camp was established by the Royal Marines in 1860, at the beginning of the joint military occupation of the island. Four of the thirty primary military buildings remain. One is open to the public and they are all described by interpretive signs. Most of the other buildings were sold by the US Army and moved away.

When the Marines left in 1872, a small detachment of soldiers from American Camp occupied the property. They left in 1874, when the US Army was withdrawn from the island. As soon as the soldiers left, the James Crook family occupied the property. They purchased some of the buildings from the Army and acquired the land through a pre-emption claim. They lived in an officer's house until it burned down, then lived in the barracks building, which is open to the public. In 1905, they moved to a new two- story house built by James and William Crook. They began the work in 1903 and completed it in 1905. James Crook was an excellent carpenter and the house shows evidence of quality construction. The National Park Service has not decided what to do with the house.

Jim Crook, Jr. was born shortly before his parents occupied the property. He did not marry and lived to be 93 years old, remaining here all his life. He made his own clothing, weaving the wool from his sheep on a home-made loom. The loom is displayed in Friday Harbor, in the courthouse lobby. He lived alone until he was quite elderly, then shared his home with his widowed sister, Mary Davis. When she died in an automobile accident in 1967, another widowed sister, Rhoda Anderson, came to live with him.

Portions of the farm were sold to the state in 1951 and 1953 for preservation and public access. The area occupied by the buildings and the British cemetery was sold to the state in 1963 for historic preservation, but the Crook family retained the right to occupy the house for rest of their lives. In 1966, seven months after Jim Crook died, Pres. Lyndon Johnson established the National Historical Park. In 1967, the state property was transferred to the federal government. Rhoda Anderson died in 1971.

The two large trees between the barracks and the garden are Big- leaf Maples. They were large trees when the Marines arrived in 1860. The tree nearest the garden used to be the largest Big-leaf Maple in the world, but it was damaged during a storm and it is now the second largest Big-leaf Maple.

Garrison Bay received its name during the military occupation. It is connected to Westcott Bay, seen earlier on the tour. Archaeological evidence indicates that, at one time, the water was one hundred feet higher than it is today. At other times, the water was so low the Straits of Juan de Fuca was reduced to a narrow stream. The nearby island is Guss Island, named for Augustus "Guss" Hoffmeister, the camp sutler (storekeeper), who raised cattle on Henry Island.

A military cemetery is on the side of Mt. Young and may be reached by a trail that begins near the restrooms. The trail is steep and requires careful attention to footing. Allow an hour to reach the cemetery and return to the parking lot. Seven Marines and a civilian are buried there. They died of drowning, accidental shooting, suicide, and diseases. For many years, the Canadian government paid Jim Crook a small stipend to maintain the cemetery. It is now maintained by the National Park Service. The trail continues to the top of of Mt. Young, which is 650 ft. above sea level.

This bay is also an important site in the history of the American Indians. The Lummi Indians lived here for over nine thousand years. They lived in longhouses, which were long, narrow buildings made of posts set in the ground and enclosed by planks. A longhouse found here in 1858, was 500 to 600 feet long and 50 to 60 feet wide. Longhouses were divided into small rooms, with one room for each family.

To continue the tour, return to the county highway and turn right. Travel 1.5 miles, then turn right at Mitchell Bay Rd.

If you wish to terminate the tour, remain on West Valley Rd. for a direct return to Friday Harbor.

Watch the forests and fields closely for a flock of wild turkeys, which were introduced by the State Game Department. They are rarely hunted and show little fear of humans. Also watch for Columbia Black-tail deer, which are native to the island. The deer are hunted and they are very shy.

The site of a circus camp can be seen along this road. At the entrance to Snug Harbor Resort, turn left and watch for a high- way warning sign for a fire station. The sign is seven-tenths of a mile beyond the resort entrance. Upon reaching the sign, look for a cleared field on the right side of the road. (If you get to the Sun- set Point Fire Station, you went too far.) The buildings and all other evidence of the circus have disappeared-- do not trespass on this private property.

For many years, the Beuller Circus spent the winters here on a large farm owned by the Beuller family. It was a one-ring circus that performed in small towns in the Northwest. The circus was transported to and from the island by freight boat. On one oc- casion, some monkeys escaped and had to be captured before the boat could land.

The circus took bankruptcy during the Great Depression of the 1930's and most of its animals and equipment were sold at auc- tion. Local farmers bought the sturdy circus wagons and con- verted them to farm use. (A few of the old wagons may still be on island farms.) Elmon A. Geneste, a local attorney who repre-

80

sented the circus, bought a monkey wagon which he kept on his farm on Orcas Island.

At the request of the circus owner, Geneste placed an ad in the local paper offering free ponies to local youngsters. Geneste's home was soon surrounded by youngsters wanting free ponies. The ponies were given to youngsters on condition that they return the ponies if the circus recalled them. The ponies went to many local youngsters and were never recalled. Most of the circus animals were sold at auction. When it was discovered that the trained mules were destined for the glue factory, Geneste repurchased them and placed them at Kwan Lama, a local resort. Geneste received two ponies and pony carts in lieu of his fee, which he gave to his children. The farm buildings used by the circus have all disappeared. This is private property--do not trespass.

Continue 3.2 miles on Mitchell Bay Rd. to San Juan County Park. Farmer Pat's Fruit Stand is on the left side of the road, about a half mile before reaching the County Park. During the summer and fall, the Threewit family sells fresh fruit, vegetables, and fruit juice from this stand. The fruit juice is popular with visitors and residents.

The San Juan County Park provides restrooms, picnic tables, drinking water, a boat ramp, a pay phone, RV hookups, and space for tent camping.

This is a pleasant place for a picnic or to walk among the trees or along the bay. The bay is popular with scuba divers. There are several explanations for the name of Smallpox Bay. One legend indicates Lummi Indians suffering from smallpox jumped in the bay to reduce their fever--then died of pneumonia. Another story indicates a steamer stopped here to discharge two sailors who had smallpox; the Indians who cared for the men caught smallpox and died from it. Still another legend indicates the bay was used to dispose of the bodies of Indians who died during an 1860 smallpox epidemic in Victoria. During the nineteenth century, the Indian population was decimated by smallpox and other diseases introduced by European and American settlers.

To continue the tour, return to the highway and turn right. The highway skirts the side of Mt. Dallas, the highest peak on the island. A two-mile section of gravel road begins beyond the park. When the road nears the water, watch for the entrance to Lime Kiln/Whale Watch Park. The park provides restrooms and drinking water. **This is the last drinking water source on the tour.**

During the late nineteenth and early twentieth century, several lime quarries were operated in this area, including the San Juan Lime Co., owned by James McCurdy and N.C. Bailey. McCurdy was a part-time postmaster here from 1879 to 1888. The quarry was later operated by the Henry Cowell family which owned substantial lime works in California and a small lime works on Orcas Island. Members of the Cowell family were minority stockholders of the Roche Harbor Lime Co. A quarry near here still supplies limestone for local construction projects.

A temporary lighthouse was built here in 1914, which was replaced in 1919 by the present structure. This was the last lighthouse in Washington to be converted to electricity, because electrical lines were not extended to this part of the island until the 1950's. The lighthouse is fully automated and is visited periodically by a technician who maintains the light and horn. The grounds, but not the lighthouse, were recently transferred to the state for a park.

Orca (killer whales) who reside in or visit these waters are frequently seen near this park. They are most frequently seen from late June through early August. Whales almost always travel in groups. When one is visible, others are usually nearby. Whales are frequently heard exhaling before they are seen. Harbor and River Seals, Harbor and Dall's Purposes, and Minke Whales are also seen here regularly. This is also an excellent place to observe water birds, including loons, grebes, terns, and gulls.

The small bay at the entrance to the park is Deadman Bay. Several legends account for the name. One legend indicates a cook at Cowell's lime works killed a man here because he complained about his breakfast. The Lummi Indians had a summer village here. Today, the bay is popular with scuba divers.

When you leave the park, drive straight ahead, but watch for traffic entering on your left. The next three miles provide stunning marine views. The body of water is the Haro Straits. On a clear day, Victoria, BC can be seen on the southern tip of Vancouver Island. The snow-capped Olympic Mountains are usually visible on the Olympic Peninsula.

During the spring and summer, the hillsides in this area are covered with California Poppies. When the flowers wilt, the seeds provide flowers for the following year. Picking the flowers reduces the number of seeds available the following year.

About 2.5 miles after leaving Lime Kiln/Whale Watch Park, watch for the Little Mountain Fire Station on the right side of the road. The old house just beyond the fire station was the home of Edgar Zeigler who had a 160 acre farm here. He remained a bachelor for many years and cared for his parents. In 1882, he married the widow, Minerva Elizabeth Cahoon Hannah. He died in 1904 and in 1913, she married another neighbor, Frank D. Sexton. Sexton died in 1929 and she died in 1954. This house has attractive scroll work over the entrance and in the gable.

A barn used to stand in the pasture on the opposite side of the road, about 100 yards beyond the Zeigler house. During prohibition, the barn had a secret room for hiding liquor smuggled from Canada. The barn was removed many years ago. This part of the island was commonly used for smuggling due to its proximity to Canada, numerous small coves, and heavy tree cover. Smugglers Cove is about two miles west of this point.

The county highway changes its name near here. This portion is called Bailer Hill Rd.

The crest of Bailer Hill is 1.2 miles from the Zeigler house. The hill and the road were named for the Bailer family who operated farms in this area. The top of Bailer Hill offers a nice view of the San Juan Valley, the richest agricultural area on the island. Settlers began arriving here in 1858, just before the joint military occupation of the island. The valley was fully settled by the end of the military occupation, in 1872. Some of the land is still owned by descendants of the early settlers. During the 1920's and 30's, much of the bottom land was planted in peas. The peas grew beautifully, but so did the weevils. The insects eventually made the crop unprofitable and the pea cannery closed, causing considerable hardship. Pea growing resumed in 1953, when George P. Jeffers converted the Friday Harbor Canning Co. to canning peas. The weevils were then controlled with pesticides. Pea growing stopped in about 1964, when the cannery closed due to financial problems.

Island farmers traditionally operated diversified farms that provided an income from several sources, including orchards, dairying, and sheep raising. Man-made fabrics reduced the demand for wool, making sheep raising unprofitable. Small dairy farms eventually proved to be inefficient, so the local creamery closed in the 1960's, forcing farmers to sell their cows at a loss. The orchards failed when island farmers were unable to compete with the large growers' cooperatives in Eastern Washington. The collective impact of these changes forced many families to leave the land. Some farms were sold for home sites and most of the rest became hobby or second-income farms.

One mile from the crest of Bailer Hill, turn right on False Bay Rd. The side trip may be omitted by continuing on Bailer Hill Rd.

The horse farm on both sides of the road is one of the largest farms on the island. Several smaller farms were combined to create this farm. The land nearest Bailer Hill Rd. was previously owned by Ivan Stock, who raised grass seed. This is a good place to watch birds. Many raptors, including a rare pair of Golden

Eagles, live in this area. The no-trespassing signs should be taken seriously, so watch the birds and horses from the road.

False Bay is one mile from the intersection of Bailer Hill and False Bay Rds. This beautiful bay is attractive to boaters. Boaters who fail to check their charts soon run aground, as the water is very shallow. During extremely low tides, the bottom is exposed almost all the way out to the entrance. The shore and bay are a nature preserve administered by the University of Washington Marine Laboratory. Visitors may enter the area, but are not permitted to collect specimens. Mike Lewis comments, "False Bay is the best shorebird habitat in the archipelago and nearly every species recorded in the San Juan Islands has been sited here."

Return to Bailer Hill Rd., then turn right.

The land on the left side of Bailer Hill Rd. was claimed by Patrick Beigin, an Irish immigrant. When he arrived in New York he was unable to find work, so he joined the Army. He was a member of the 9th Infantry, Company D, under Capt. George E. Pickett, when the company was sent to San Juan Island in July 1869. After completing his enlistment, he remained on the island. He built a small cabin and began clearing the land and planting crops. He fell in love with an Indian princess from southern Alaska. Her father did not approve of the marriage, so they eloped. The original log house was replaced by a large house in about 1908 or 1910. The large house burned early in the 1920's and was replaced by a small house built higher on the hill.

After Patrick Beigin died, their son William acquired the farm. William died in a hunting accident in 1931 the farm was acquired by Ray Fleming, a relative. It is no longer owned by the Beigin descendants, but a great grandson owns a nearby farm.

The first two houses on the left side of the road were built or moved there in the last fifteen years. The third house on the left side of the road was built in the 1920's by William Beigin to replace the house that burned down. Notice the large, unpainted building in front of the house. The tall portion of the building is a water tower. The upper part of the building contained a water tank which supplied water to the house and barn. Before electricity was available to operate farm water systems, many farms had water towers similar to this one. The tanks were usually filled by a windmill. Many water towers have fallen or have been removed.

Two of the houses on the other side of the road were moved here during the 1980's. The small house with the red roof was moved here from West Seattle. The larger house on the left was moved here from Friday Harbor to make way for a shopping center. It was built on Argyle St. in the 1890's for Mr. & Mrs. B.O. Cahail. Mr. Cahail was an officer in the bank and was the County Treasurer. Their son was the mayor of Friday Harbor in the mid-1940's. A grandson is now the mayor of Friday Harbor.

Bailer Hill Rd. curves to the left to become Douglas Rd. This road offers and attractive panorama of the valley and the three highest peaks, from left to right, Mt. Dallas (1,080 ft.), Cady Mountain (900 ft.), and Mt. Young (650 ft.).

After passing Short Rd., notice the large Garry Oak trees on the right side of the road. In the mid-nineteenth century, oak trees were so numerous that the San Juan Valley was named Oak Valley. They are numerous here, but they are scarce elsewhere on the island. The hill on the right side of the road is called Oak Ridge.

At the end of Douglas Rd., turn right on San Juan Valley Rd. The tour ends as you enter Friday Harbor. Continue straight ahead to return to the starting point of the tour.

As you enter Friday Harbor, watch the speed limit.

86

TOUR THREE: A WALKING TOUR OF

DOWNTOWN FRIDAY HARBOR

Distance: One mile. A map follows page 5.

This tour was designed for walking. Heavy traffic and a lack of parking spaces makes it difficult to use cars and bicycles on this tour.

Start the tour in front of the ferry terminal building. The Friday Harbor Packing Company once stood on the area occupied by the Cannery Landing, and the condominiums. The cannery was built in 1890 and became a major local industry. George P. Jeffers bought it 1945 from Schultz & Martell. When fish canning became unprofitable in the 1950's, Jeffers converted it to a pea cannery. When the price of peas fell in the 1960's, it was sold to a fishermen's cooperative. When that failed, the buildings stood vacant. It was demolished in the 1980's to make way for the Cannery Village complex.

Cannery House, the yellow house across the street from the terminal building, is the only remnant of the cannery. It was built in 1909 as the home for the cannery owner. Mr. & Mrs. Jeffers lived in the home from 1945 until they died. Several people say the house is haunted; family members think it is Mr. Jeffers' benign spirit who walks up the porch steps in the evening and paces during the night, as he did during his final illness. When Mrs. Jeffers died in 1973, her daughter lived upstairs and used the first floor for an art gallery. In 1978, the house was sold to David Dobson, who added the gables and the deck. He used the first floor for a restaurant and the upper floors for apartments. Several years ago, the building inspector closed the business for code violations. The issue is now in litigation. The space occupied by East St. used to

87

be the side yard of the house. For many years, a deep ravine ran between the house and the commercial buildings on Spring St. The ravine has been filled and the deck on the side of the house occupies that space.

The ferry holding lanes replaced several old buildings. A small cannery office stood near the entrance to the present florist's shop. A two-story boarding house for migrant workers stood south of Cannery House. A wooden water tower stood by the boarding house.

King's slaughter house was a one-story wooden building about half way up the block, behind the boarding house. It was built in 1914 as a farmers' cooperative creamery. When a larger creamery was built in 1924, Lyle King bought the old creamery and converted it to a slaughter house. The business was operated by his son, Carl, who eventually acquired the property.

At the top of the ferry lanes stood an old, two-story house built for Mr. & Mrs. Charles McKay. McKay was one of the first Americans to arrive on the island in 1858. He raised the US flag at the protest rally on July 4, 1859, he served as a county commissioner, and was active in island politics. During his later years, he operated the Pioneer's Blacksmith Shop behind this house. The house was later occupied by Mr. & Mrs. Carl King.

The cannery office, the boarding house, the water tower, the slaughter house, and the McKay house were demolished in 1978 to make way for the ferry holding lanes.

Walk along the waterfront toward Mojo's Restaurant. The oldest extant photograph of Friday Harbor shows a small building on pilings in this location, with a dock extending from the shore on the north side of the building. This is probably the site of a warehouse and dock built in the late 1870's by Joseph Sweeny. Sweeny bought the land in this area in 1876, cleared the trees, and built a combination general store and post office. The warehouse and dock was added a little later. In 1934, the dock and warehouse became as a Coast Guard station. It was later used as the Pier 1 Restaurant. By the mid-twentieth century, it was badly deteriorated and was considered for demolition, but Roman and April Sobinsky renovated it for a curio shop. It was later converted to a restaurant. The building burned once and has been expanded several times, but parts of the old building remain.

SPRING IS A FUNNY NAME FOR A STREET

Spring St. is the oldest street in Friday Harbor. It began in 1873 as a dirt trail with a few little shacks on either side of the trail. It got its name from a natural spring which bubbled from the ground in the middle of the street. When the water level dropped, a pump was installed at the spring with a watering trough for horses. Children were sent to the well to pump buckets of water for bathing, drinking, and cleaning. They also pumped water for the horses, cows, and chickens. The well was removed in the 1920's, after the town water system was installed. The well site was paved over, but water continued to seep from the ground, undermining the pavement. The problem was solved by diverting the water to a culvert. Today, the spring water flows into the harbor, just below Circle Park.

Continue along the waterfront to Circle Park. This little park began early in this century as a circular patch of grass, surrounded by boulders. The elm trees were planted early in this century. The World War I memorial was added in 1921 by the Women's Study

Club. The flagpole formerly stood a block up the hill, in the center of Spring and First Sts. It was knocked over one night by an errant driver, so it was moved to the park. When the new ferry dock was built in 1978, it was suggested that the park be removed to facilitate traffic movement. The Women's Study Club and other organizations fought to retain the park. To improve traffic flow, a bulkhead was built to provide additional street space between the park and the harbor. An old photograph of the park hangs in the San Juan Doughnut Shop, two blocks up the street.

The Downrigger restaurant stands near the site of the old ferry terminal. The Black Ball Line, which became the Washington State Ferries in 1951, introduced ferry service here in 1927. Before that, transportation was offered by packet boats, called "the mosquito fleet." These small, wood-burning boats carried freight, mail, and passengers up and down the sound. Loading a car required placing planks, called "transfer boards," between the dock and the forward deck of the boat. The car was then pushed or driven onto the boat. During rough weather, cars were tied down to keep them from falling overboard. As the demand for automobile transportation grew, some boats were modified to carry several cars per trip. Eventually, many boats were rebuilt so the main deck could be loaded entirely with cars. As auto traffic increased, the transfer boards were replaced by adjustable slips, similar to those used today.

The yellow building across the street is particularly interesting. Portions of that building may be the oldest commercial building in town. In 1883, the 50 x 100 foot lot on the corner was sold at public auction for $300. The deed included "tenements, hereditaments, and appurtenances thereunto belonging or in anywise appertaining." That probably included the building. The buyer was Israel Katz, who operated a general store at San Juan Town, on the south end of the island. Katz used this building to buy potatoes and other produce for resale throughout the area. Katz named this building the Friday Harbor Produce Exchange. The following year, Katz sold the building and the adjoining lot to William H. Higgins. Higgins was a carpenter who also supplied cord wood to the San Juan Lime Co. It is not known how Higgins used the building. After that, the building had several owners and passed though a sheriff's auction in 1892. The building was sold in 1895 to Jack Douglas, who converted it to the Saloon Best. Local people called it the "lower tavern." The taverns up the street were the "middle tavern" and the "upper tavern". A hitching rail stood on the waterfront side of this building. Early in this century, Douglas installed the large windows in the front of the building. The building later served as a grocery store. In 1930, it became the Moose Lodge. The building was sold in 1969 to the 1901 Corp., which converted it to an art gallery and bookstore.

The rear part of the building was added early in this century as the Newport Pool Room, which the Moose Lodge used as a dance hall. The large windows were added in the 1970's, when the dance hall was converted to a restaurant. The arcade was added in the 1960's to enclose an alleyway between two buildings. The next building was built early in this century, when it was known as Delmonico's Restaurant. It was used as a grocery store, then became the "lower tavern".

Cross Spring St. at the intersection. The vacant lot which is now used for a parking lot, T-shirt shop, and moped rentals was the site of Sweeny Mercantile, the first store in Friday Harbor. The first building was built in 1876 or 1877. The business was described in 1901 as follows:

This institution stands as the results of the labors of Mr. Joseph Sweeny, who is the pioneer merchant of this place. The store room is 30x70 feet in size, and here is carried a full and complete line of general merchandise, including foreign and domestic dry goods, notions and ladies' furnishings, fancy and staple groceries, builders and contractors' supplies, hardware and all kinds of goods of a general useful and ornamental nature, candies, nuts, tobacco and cigars. This firm also deals in

hay, feed, grain, lumber, doors, sash, blinds, paints, etc.
and all kinds of country produce is bought and sold.
Mr. Sweeny in connection with the store maintains a
wharf and warehouse, and is prepared to buy and store
wool.

The business prospered during the 1890's and early part of
this century. After the business closed, one building became a
warehouse and the other one became a theater for silent films.
The deteriorating buildings were demolished in the 1930's. In
April, 1930, a proposal was presented to build a seven-story, fifty-
room brick hotel on this site. The ground floor was to include a
two-story lobby, plus a coffee shop, dining room, cigar store, drug
store, and two additional shops. The mezzanine floor was to include three suites, a private dining room, and a lounge. It was not
built because the developer could not obtain financing during the
Depression.

In 1954, the Garden Club converted part of the vacant lot to
a park. Many of the plants were killed by a severe frost and the
club replanted the area in 1962. In the 1970's a developer wanted
to build an apartment here, but the plan was defeated by citizen
opposition. The lot was recently the focus of another legal dispute. A developer wanted to build a four-story motel here, but the
plans were blocked by groups opposed to the project. Many who
opposed the plan want to use the lot for a park. That issue has not
been resolved yet.

The blue real-estate office served for many years as a barber
shop, operated variously by A. Stoliker, Art McKay (son of
pioneer, Charles McKay), Jack McCutchon, and Jake Duyff. The
barber shop also served as a collection and distribution point for
the Pacific Steam Laundry of Whatcom (later Bellingham). The
upper floor was an apartment which was occupied for many years
by the McCutchons. The building was purchased in about 1970 by
John Holm who converted it to a restaurant. The building was
later purchased by Joe Fanjul, who converted it to a real estate of-

fice. The old barber's back bar, with a bullet hole in the mirror, is now in the Front Street Restaurant, in the former Newport Pool Room. A boardwalk provides access to several small shops at the rear of the building.

The building on the other side of the boardwalk is the San Juan Hotel. It was built in 1884 by William Douglas, and was known as the Douglas House. Douglas was the second merchant in Friday Harbor, and the one who introduced the back-room bar to Friday Harbor. His store and bar was across the street, but the exact location is unknown. The hotel was later purchased by James Ross who called it the Bay View Hotel. Patrick Welsh bought the hotel in 1901 and renamed it the Tourists' Hotel Annex. He operated it in conjunction with the Tourists' Hotel, a block away. In about 1911, the local telephone company moved its switchboard to the hotel. In the 1950's, the building fell into disrepair and was restored in the 1970's by John Holm. When the hotel was new, water for drinking and bathing was pumped from a well in the back yard. The hand pump in the hotel's back yard may be seen from the entrance to Nieman's Fine Gifts. This may not be the original pump, but it is probably the location of the original well. When the street was widened and raised, the original front porch was removed and several large windows on the lower floor were replaced by smaller windows.

The building on the corner was built in 1892 by San Juan Trading Co., owned by M.R. Noftsger and Norman E. Churchill. In 1901, Churchill bought out is partner. At the turn of the century, the store had a grand facade facing Spring St., with an entrance in the center of the building. The building has been used as a tavern for many years. The small real estate office on the lower floor had many previous occupants, including the the G.B. Driggs Grocery Store and the Sherwood & Gagner Barbershop.

The town's flagpole used to stand in the center of this intersection. Cross Spring St. to the grocery store. The present building occupies the site of the old St. Charles Hotel, an early-day bordello. It was replaced around the turn of the century by a combination pool hall and confectionery store, a steam laundry, and a barber shop. After World War II, they were replaced by the present building.

Cross First Street to the Coldwell Banker San Juan Properties office. This was the site of the second courthouse, which was built in 1883. The courthouse was moved up the street in about 1906 and this building was built in 1907 for the San Juan County Bank. The bank opened in 1883, ten years after the town was founded. A picture of this building, taken shortly before the windows were installed, may be seen in the San Juan Doughnut Shop, a block up the street. In 1978, the bank moved to a new building and the old bank was converted to its present use.

The National Park Service Headquarters next to the old bank was the home of the *Friday Harbor Journal*. The paper began in 1906 as a Democratic alternative to the Republican *Islander*. A corner of the building served as the US Customs Office when O.H. Culver was the publisher and the deputy customs collector. The *Journal* outgrew this building and was moved to its present location on Tucker Ave. The old newspaper office was purchased by the bank with the intention of using it for additional bank offices. The bank did not implement that plan, but built a new bank building.

Notice the three buildings across the street. The Ross Building on the right served for many years as Tulloch's Hardware Store, with the upper floor used as the Maple House Hotel. The hardware store had a number of owners. In recent years, the windows on the upper floor were shuttered and the exterior of the building was covered with blue, sheet-metal roofing. In 1986, the building and the hardware business were purchased by Vern Howard, who operates King's Market. In 1987 the building was remodeled to its present appearance.

The two-story, block building in the center of the block was built in about 1904 by L.B. Carter, a prominent local merchant. It later served as Roark's Dry Good Store. Mr. Roark was Mr.

Carter's son-in-law and previously managed the dry goods department of Carter's store. The building is now owned by Vern
Howard and will eventually be remodeled to harmonize with the
Ross Building on the right. The spring that gave Spring St. it's
name used to stand in the middle of Spring St. in this block.

The one-story grocery store at the corner of Spring and
Second Sts. occupies the site of two old stores. The left part of the
building was built in 1948 by Lyle King to replace an older building that burned down. It occupies the site of a general store
operated by G.B. Driggs and Pete Jensen, then by Pete Jensen,
and later by William "Alfie" Middleton. The right side of the one-
story building occupies the site of Mason's Shoe Store. After the
shoe store closed, the building was demolished and the grocery
store was expanded into that space.

Walk up the street to the Royal Theater. The theater opened
on July 4, 1915, as the Fribor Theater. It was designed for silent
movies and live performances. It is used today for films and
amateur performances. In 1959, Milton and Lee Bave purchased
the theater and restored it for use by MADD (Music, Art, Drama,
and Dance), a community arts organization. The scrollwork on
the front of the building was added by the Baves. The building was
sold to the manager in 1974, who later sold it to an investor.

The San Juan Doughnut Shop, next to the theater, is a
popular place to exchange local gossip. Several excellent
photographs of early-day Friday Harbor are displayed there. The
building was used for many years as a physicians office. The last
physician to use the office was Dr. Malcolm Heath, who received
national publicity in the 1960's as the "Flying Doctor of the San
Juans." Dr. Heath served the entire county and flying to his
patients was quicker and easier than traveling by ferry or private
boat. After Dr. Heath moved his office to the medical center (the
present Courthouse Annex), the building became a barber shop.

The elegant two-story store next to the doughnut shop served
for many years as a dentist's office for Dr. Roger Loring. The

second floor, now used as a shop, was built as a residence. The Italianate brackets on the facade were added in the 1960's, when the building was restored.

The barber shop next door was built by Dr. Loring as a second dentist's office. It has had many uses, including a farrier's (horse shoeing) shop. a boutique, and a veterinarian's office. Bear, the barber's dog, accepts praise and dog biscuits from anyone.

The house next to the barber shop was built in about 1877 for John H. Bowman, a prominent merchant and politician. (When Bowman first moved to Friday Harbor, he lived in Warbass' shanty.) The house stands on the upper end of the fifty-six acre tract Bowman purchased in 1876, shortly after he became the County Assessor. (This event is described in Chapter 4.) This is one of the older residences in town and features a fine display of Victorian scrollwork. For many years the house was owned by Ida Nichols and it is frequently identified as the Nichols house. The house originally stood on a large lot, but most of the property was subdivided by Mrs. Nichols. The small houses on Nichols Ave. occupy the old Nichols property.

Return to the Royal Theater and cross Spring St. to the Friday Harbor Drug Store. The store began in about 1900 and the first known owner was Dr. C. Tager, who owned drug stores in Arlington and Friday Harbor. The first known pharmacist was Mrs. Alice L. Summers, who probably worked for Dr. Tager. Dr. George S. Wright bought the pharmacy in 1902 and hired his cousin, Leon L. Little, to work there. After returning from military service in World War I, Leon Little and Albert M. Nash bought the store from Dr. Wright. Nash soon bought Little's interest in the store. Nash was succeeded by his son, Al, Jr., who continues to operate the store. He is assisted by many friends and family members. Until 1972, this was the only pharmacy in the county.

The store has been in at least four locations on Spring St. It probably began on the ground floor of the two-story section of the store. The two-story section of the building originally stood a block up the street. It was moved here in 1972, where it was used as a gift shop. The french doors, the porch, and the pillars were added after the building was moved. The pillars were salvaged from the old high school when it was demolished. The Nash family purchased the two-story building when they acquired the Hallmark Card dealership.

The drug store is worth a visit. The merchandise arrangement is unique and customers sometimes need help finding what they want. When asked why the merchandise is arranged as it is, one exasperated young clerk responded, "That's where they put it the first time and its been there ever since." Another employee responded, "You must understand, this is a small-town drug store that never grew up" Many residents use the store's monthly sale to stock-up on vitamins, soup, shampoo, chili, notebooks, tuna, toothpaste, toilet tissue, and other necessities. The store has a large and loyal following of residents who feel indebted to the Nash family for favors received in time of need.

From the drug store, go up Spring St. to a complex of blue buildings with white trim. The central part of this complex is a house built for Dr. George S. Wright, a graduate of Yale Medical School. His office occupied a one story building next to the house, which has been removed. After Dr. Wright died, the house became a mortuary operated by Harry King. It stood for many years between the drug store and the hardware store, on the site of Jeri's Mall. The mortuary closed in 1972, and the building was moved up the street and attached to Creamery House, a one- story home occupied by the creamery manager. Creamery House was converted to a restaurant. It was destroyed by fire and was later replaced by the present restaurant building. The narrow, two-story structure on the right side of the complex was added in 1987. The tree in front of the restaurant is a Camperdown Elm, which stood in front of Creamery House.

Continue up the street. The lumber yard was built in 1924 as a cooperative creamery operated by the San Juan County Dairymen's Association. When the association took bankruptcy, the Browne family bought the building and remodeled it for their lumber and hardware business. The business previously occupied the old pea cannery, near the present Port of Friday Harbor.

Continue up the street. The service station and garage is known locally as "the upper station." It was built in 1937 by the San Juan Island Grange, a nonprofit farmers' organization. The Farm Store was a nonprofit feed store, hardware store, and service station. A food freezing plant was installed later. In 1946, the building was leased to Baker and Fairweather as a commercial farm store. In 1964, the building was leased to Standard Oil Company. The garage was added by the oil company.

The Little Store, on the other side of the street, is known as "the lower station." In 1906, the old courthouse was moved here to become Dr. Victor J. Capron's office and hospital. Dr. Capron died in 1934 and the medical building was demolished and replaced by a combination automobile dealership and service station. After World War II, it was a Kaiser-Frazer dealership, then a Chevrolet dealership. The building was substantially modified to create the present clothing store and service station.

Continue up Spring St. The large, wooden building on the end of block was built in 1897 as the Friday Harbor Presbyterian Church. It was expanded in 1922 and was replaced in 1988 by the church across the street. The old church is being converted to offices for architects, artists, and related professionals. The old church bell was removed and it will be installed in the new church.

At the corner, notice the large, two-story house across the corner. It was built in about 1916 by Elijah H. Nash, a commercial fisherman. Nash is said to have built the house after an especially good year of fishing. He served from 1921 to 1933 as the postmaster. The house has had several owners--all members of the Nash family.

Turn right on Blair St. and look for the Blair House Bed & Breakfast on the left side of the street. This was the second house

98

built for Mr. & Mrs. John H. Bowman. The first Bowman home, the Nichols house, was described earlier on this tour. This home was later occupied by Dr. & Mrs. Victor J. Capron. Dr. Capron was the physician at Roche Harbor who later moved his practice to Friday Harbor. It was later owned by Mr. & Mrs. Charles Schmidt. Schmidt was a prominent local attorney. The house was recently converted to a bed and breakfast.

At the post office, turn right on Park St. The courthouse at the end of the block was built in 1908 to replace the wooden courthouse on Spring St. When the courthouse addition was being built, the engineers discovered the foundation of the old building was unsafe and the building was evacuated. The county offices are housed in the courthouse addition in other buildings until the county commissioners decide what to do with the old building. Repairing the foundation and other preservation measures would cost $200,000 more than demolishing the old building and building an equal amount of new space. Some say the old building was badly built by a dishonest contractor and is not worth saving. Others want to save the building, but they have not raised enough money to do so. The building remains empty until the county commissioners decide to restore it or demolish it. An interesting historical display may be viewed on the first floor of the courthouse addition.

Go down Court St., the street in front of the old courthouse. The green building to the left of the American Legion Building was built as a Methodist Church by the Rev. Andrew J. McNemee. McNemee invested his own money and labor to build a Methodist church in Port Townsend. Shortly after it was finished, he was dismissed because the congregation wanted a married minister. He was so poor he couldn't buy a ticket to leave town, so the International Order of Good Templars, a temperance lodge, bought him a ticket to Portland, where his brother gave him a new suit and enough money to reach his next assignment, the San Juans. After receiving a less-than-cordial welcome on Lopez Island, he went to San Juan Island, where he was hospitably received by a few Methodists. McNemee had difficulty building a congregation because of his uncompromising views on temperance and because most church-going people were already committed to the Presbyterian and Roman Catholic churches. A church member donated a plot of land in Friday Harbor and McNemee cleared two acres of brush and second-growth timber for the church. He built the church during the winter of 1889-1890, begging materials, labor, and money from all directions. When the church was finished, he was personally liable for $360 for materials. Shortly after the building was dedicated, he was transferred to Edison, WA. Again, he was so poor he had to borrow money to pay for his trip. It took him many years to pay for the churches he built in Port Townsend and Friday Harbor. McNemee was succeeded by several ministers, most of whom left after one year. One minister who remained for several years was the Rev. Thomas L. Dyer. His income from the collection plate would not support a wife and ten children, so he taught at a country school and worked as a commercial fisherman. When returning from fishing trips, he frequently towed a drift log to the sawmill to sell for a dollar. Much of the family's food came from their garden, milk cow, and chickens. Eventually, the parish closed and the building was sold in 1911 to the Women's Study Club. In 1975, the club sold it to the Grange, but retained the right to hold its monthly meetings here without paying rent.

The building has been substantially modified. It was built with a small bell tower at the right end of the roof, which was removed while the Study Club owned the building. The bell was later used as a dinner bell on a local farm and now stands outside the San Juan Island Historical Museum. The Study Club also added the fireplace and center entrance. Recently, the Grange added a wing containing an entrance, restrooms, and kitchen. This is a popular place for family, club, and church events. It has been used on several occasions for benefit performances to raise money to help needy families pay medical bills.

The building on the other side of the American Legion was built in 1892 as the Odd Fellows Hall. It was used as a court room in 1895 for the trial of Richard Straub for the murder of Leon

Lanterman. Straub was the only person executed in San Juan County. The building was used for a temperance sermon on May 9, 1910, by the Rev. Billy Sunday. On the following day, the voters passed a referendum to make the county dry. The lodge surrendered its charter in about 1955, due to a lack of members. The remaining members transferred to the Eastsound Odd Fellows Lodge. The building stood empty for several years and there was talk of demolishing the building. Milton and Lee Bave, bought the building in 1960 to protect it. (They previously purchased and restored the Royal Theater.) They used the lower floor for historic pageants and the upper floor for a youth club. Later, they gave the Cetalogical Society free rent to the upper floor for its office and the Whale Museum. The society is currently acquiring the building from Mrs. Bave. The Whale Museum is the only museum in the US devoted to natural history of live whales. The museum is fascinating and visitors are welcome.

Walk down First St. The small restaurant at the corner of First and West Sts. is one of the oldest buildings in Friday Harbor. It was the home of Mr. & Mrs. A. C. Brown; Mr. Brown was one of the founders of the Seventh- Day Adventist Church. He operated the sawmill at McDonald's Beach. The house was later converted to a commercial building. There is a strong probability that the part nearest the corner was erected at American Camp by the US Army. When the Army left in 1884, most of the military buildings were moved to other parts of the island. Army records indicate the buildings were sold, but local legends indicate the small buildings were "liberated" when the Army wasn't looking. Some buildings at American Camp were sold and the property-dispersal officer may have reported all the buildings were sold to avoid any unpleasant encounters with his superior officer. Historians with the National Park Service cannot find enough evidence to certify that this was a military building from American Camp, but they acknowledge, unofficially, that the story is probably true.

Turn left on West St. The restaurant at the end of the street was a house built by Jack Douglas, who owned the Saloon Best.

This house has been used as a restaurant for many years and has been enlarged to accommodate a commercial kitchen.

From the mini-park at the end of West St., notice Brown Island, on the other side of the harbor. The island has had an interesting history. It was named in 1841 by Commander Charles Wilkes, of the US Navy, probably for John G. Brown, a mathematical instrument maker. The island is now an exclusive residential subdivision, but it has had other uses. During local-option prohibition, Jack Douglas moved Saloon Best to a shack on Brown Island. His customers had to row to the island for a drink, but his business remained legal and prosperous. A few years later, during county-wide prohibition, Sheriff Ed Delaney seized an illegal tavern operating in a shack on the island. The liquor was locked in the local jail, but some local boys broke into the jail and took six cases of the liquor. When the Sheriff discovered the loss, he began looking for sick boys, and soon identified the thieves. Five cases of liquor were returned.

The building on the other side of the street was built in 1916 for a Ford dealership operated by Calvin Lightheart and George Franck. Today, the automobile showroom is occupied by beauty and cleaning shops and the garage is occupied by a restaurant.

Continue down the hill on First St. The hotel on the other side of the street was built in 1891 by Patrick Welsh, who called it the Tourists' Hotel. The hotel was eloquently described in a 1901 newspaper supplement

A metropolitan institution and an establishment which is of great credit to San Juan county and Friday Harbor is the Tourists' Hotel, which was built and established in 1891, by Patrick Welsh, and is constructed upon lines of the modern hostelry and is conducted in a manner well worthy of and fully equal to the importance which it holds in the community. Everything in and pertain-

5. Odd Fellows Lodge/Whale Museum.

6. St. Francis Roman Catholic Church.

ing to the place is kept in the most cleanly and attractive manner, and the care and attention shown the guests is pleasing and satisfactory.

Here is a fine, large building, fitted and furnished throughout in comfort and cleanness. Water is piped to each floor. A ladies' reception room and large verandah faces toward the ocean and incoming and outgoing vessels can be seen. In the cuisine, everything is first-class in every respect and care is taken to serve only the very best and freshest supplies prepared with cleanliness and dispatch. The culinary and dining room service is all that could be desired and more than expected in a place the size of Friday Harbor. .... Mr. Welsh conducts a bar and pool room, wherein he dispenses all kinds of domestic and imported liquors, whiskey, ale, beer, gin, wine, porter and other liquid refreshments and carries good brands of cigars.

The bar and pool room were on the left side of the main floor and were commonly called the "upper tavern." The dining room and kitchen occupied the rest of the main floor. The ladies' lounge was in the front corner of the second floor, above the bar. In later years, the ladies' lounge was used as a dentist's office. Between 1901 and 1907, a livery barn was built in back of the hotel. The original verandah was removed when the street was widened and raised. The building was restored in the 1960's by Bob Carter.

The newer buildings on the other side of the street occupy the site of a two-story produce warehouse used in conjunction with Churchill's store. The store is now occupied by the tavern.

Continue on First St. Sunshine Alley eplaced Friday Creek which ran through a deep ravine. Early settlers used the ravine as a trash dump. Outhouses stood on the edge of the ravine. The creek now runs through a and empties into the harbor near the ferry terminal. Sunshine Gallery, an artists' cooperative, is in the basement of the old bank building.

The other side of First St. was once occupied by a series of buildings that have been removed. The two-story building on the right occupies the site of two old buildings. The corner building was a mortuary built by Elias F. Harpst in about 1880. The building was used later as a dry cleaning shop, then as a fish store. The building was burned in 1978 by an arsonist. The Harpst residence, which stood behind the mortuary, was moved to the fair grounds, where it serves as the Scout Building. A.D. Conway's Blacksmith Shop stood beside the mortuary.

Next to that was a three-story livery barn operated by Warren Dightman. The stable was below street level and the carriages and wagons were stored at street level. Hay was stored in the loft. Aleck J. Lightheart's livery barn stood on the other side of Friday Creek. It was later acquired by Warren Dightman and the two livery barns were operated as a single business. Mr. & Mrs. Lightheart then managed the Tourists' Hotel and Livery Stable, up the street.

Continue on First St. The large, two-story house on the corner of First and A Sts. was built late in the nineteenth century for Mr. & Mrs. Norman E. Churchill. Mr. Churchill was an elegant gentleman who wore formal dress for dinner. (He was a distant cousin to the Duke of Marlborough.) Churchill operated a general store in the building now occupied by Herb's Tavern. During the 1960's this house served as Kellog's Rooming House. It now houses small offices and shops. The owner of the property plans to build a motel on this site. It is unknown if the house will be moved or demolished.

This is the end of the tour. The starting point of the tour is one block away, at the bottom of East St.

TOUR FOUR: THE UNIVERSITY OF
WASHINGTON MARINE LABORATORY

Distance: 1.4 miles. This is an excellent destination for a walk or a short bicycle ride.

Directions: From Second and Spring Sts., in downtown Friday Harbor, go up Second St. to the top of the hill. At the end of Second St., turn left on Guard St. Go one block, then turn right on Tucker Ave. Go 4/10 of a mile on Tucker Ave., then turn right on University Rd. After crossing the speed bump, turn right and park in the parking lot. Fernald Laboratory is the large building facing the parking lot.

> Animals are prohibited on the property to preserve the biological preserve. Do not permit your dog, cat, or other animal to leave your vehicle.

The Friday Harbor Marine Labs are operated by the University of Washington as a research center. The waters in this area are a rich source of important marine species. To take advantage of this valuable natural resource, the University established the Puget Sound Biological Station in Friday Harbor in 1910. In 1921, the federal government transferred a 484-acre military reserve to the University of Washington for a marine research station. The laboratory received substantial financial assistance during that period from the Rockefeller Foundation. Today, there are six major buildings on the campus to house laboratories, classrooms, a dining room, and a library. Several homes and dormitories on the campus accommodate the staff, students, and visiting scholars.

In the summer, hundreds of students come here to attend graduate-level classes or work on their dissertations.

This is a quiet and attractive place to visit, but visitors should recognize that important research is conducted here which must not be disturbed. The breakthrough in the search for the cure for cancer or heart disease may result from research at this laboratory. Visitors may enter Fernald Laboratory to view public exhibits in the upper and lower lobbies. Public restrooms are available inside the entrance of Fernald Laboratory. Visitors must not enter other rooms without permission. All of the other buildings are closed to visitors.

The bluff south of the main building offers a splendid view of the harbor, Brown Island, San Juan Channel, and Mount Baker. The area is inhabited by many rabbits. It is unclear when or how they were introduced to the island. The State Game Department classifies them as escaped domestic animals; rabbit hunting is not regulated by the Game Department, but it is prohibited on the university grounds. During the 1970's, most of the rabbits died from an unknown cause. The rabbits seen here are part of a small group of survivors.

The dock below Fernald Laboratory is used by research vessels, including the *Nugget,* which is usually moored there. Visitors may NOT walk on the dock unless they are accompanied by laboratory personnel. The structure built over the water is a water intake which supplies salt water to specimen tanks. Local sailors call it "the cantilever." Do NOT walk or climb on this structure.

The old-growth forest surrounding the buildings is worthy of a visit. Many Columbia Black-tail Deer live in the forest. Visitors may walk in the forest if they take suitable steps to preserve the habitat:

1. Do not permit pets to enter the biological preserve.

2. Do not litter.

106

3. Do not collect rocks, sticks, plants, insects, etc

4. Do not hunt or trap animals.

5. Do not light fires.

TOUR FIVE: JACKSON BEACH, WITH A SCENIC RETURN TRIP VIA TURN POINT

Directions: From downtown Friday Harbor, go up Spring St. to the Y intersection with Argyle St. Turn left on Argyle and continue to the edge of town. Turn left onto Turn Point Rd., then turn right onto Jackson Beach Rd.

Distance: 1.3 miles.

Facilities: A sandy beach, boat-launch ramp, and volleyball standards (bring your own net). Restrooms and drinking water are NOT available in the park.

This beach, is named for John Jackson, who built the cannery, but some older residents call it Argyle Spit. It was recently donated to the county and it is operated jointly by the county and the Port of Friday Harbor. It is a low sandy spit studded with driftwood. It is a popular place for picnics, volleyball, sunbathing, walking, beachcombing, bird watching, boat watching, and driftwood gathering. Firewood cutting is permitted. The county and the port district maintain the park, but have no plans to improve it.

The beach is a good place to observe large tug boats maneuvering gravel barges at the nearby gravel pit. Most of the gravel is hauled to Canada. During the commercial fishing season, fishing boats and tenders can be seen unloading at the cannery at the end of the spit. (Fishing boats are described on page 56) The cannery is on private property which is closed to the public. It was built during World War II, to smoke and can salmon.

108

The water between the sandy spit and the rocky shore is Argyle Lagoon. Some older residents call it Sawmill Bay, because two sawmills once stood on the far shore. The lagoon is a nature preserve administered by the University of Washington Marine Laboratory. Do not enter the nature preserve.

A five mile scenic trip to Friday Harbor is available via Turn Point. To take the scenic route, turn right at the park entrance and drive through the gravel pit. (The road through the gravel pit is a public road.) On the other side of the gravel pit, the road is paved again. The road follows the shoreline around Turn Point and returns to downtown Friday Harbor. This route is well suited for hiking or bicycling, but there are no tourist facilities along the way.

TOUR 6: JAKLE'S LAGOON NATURE TRAIL

The trail is in the American Camp National Historical Park. It begins at the parking lot just east of the intersection of Cattle Point Rd. and Picketts Lane. The trail is nine tenths of a mile long. It is on fairly level ground and does not require strenuous activity. The most difficult grade is clearly identified and an alternate return route is identified.

To enter the nature trail, step across the chain barrier at the end of the parking lot and follow the trail. Watch for small numbered stakes on either side of the trail. The first marker is about one hundred yards beyond the chain barrier. The following description of the flora along the trail is reproduced, with permission, from a guide written for the San Juan Horticultural Society. The description is based on the flora seen in the spring, which may be somewhat different than the plants seen at other times of the year.

After crossing the chain barrier, notice:

OREGON GRAPE, *Berberis aquifolium,* which reminds us of English holly, is a shrub that may reach a height of two meters and inhabits roadsides, brushy areas, and open woods. It has compound leaves. Each leaflet is bright shiny green with needle- sharp points. Bright yellow flowers cluster at the apex of the plant in early spring. Fall brings dark blue berries. They are too sour for pleasant eating, but they make excellent jelly. Yellow roots and inner bark can be used as dye.

FILAREE or STORK'S BILL, *Erodium cicutarium*, is a ground-hugging rosette of fern-like leaves with lavender-rose, five-petaled flowers which are about one centimeter across. The

110

immature fruit resembles a stork's bill. Filaree is an Old World introduction.

STAKE 1

DOUGLAS FIR, *Pseudotsuga menziesii,* is not a true fir. New to early Northwest explorers, it was often misnamed pine, spruce or hemlock. Its scientific name *Pseudotsauga* (false hemlock) reflects this confusion. The Latin name, *Menziesii,* honors Alexander Menzies, the first European to describe the tree (in 1791). Menzies was a naturalist who accompanied Captain George Vancouver on his voyages to the Northwest. David Douglas, another early explorer-botanist, was honored with its English name. The cone, or fruit, which shelters the seeds, hangs down. Its three-pointed bracts are sometime described as tiny three-pronged pitchforks. Early-spring buds are shiny reddish brown and pointed. Young trees have smooth gray-brown bark; older trees develop coarse, heavy, deeply fissured bark which helps protect the tree during forest fires. the Douglas fir is one of the Northwest's most valued trees. It furnishes lumber, plywood, paper pulp and Christmas trees.

PACIFIC SANICULA, *Sanicula crassicaulis,* has leaves of dark green which are three-lobed, toothed, and may measure ten centimeters across. The stems grow thirty to fifty centimeters tall, Clusters of small yellow flowers tip the stems. The base of the flower stems has small, pointed leaves.

YELLOW PAINT, *Lepraria candelaris,* is a yellow lichen which tints the bark of trees with a bright yellow powder. Several good examples of the lichen occur to the right of the trail on Douglas fir trees.

MINER'S LETTUCE, *Montia perfoliata,* has elongated leaves at the base. What appears to be a single leaf encircles the tender stem and forms a cup to hold a nosegay of tiny white flowers. As the name suggests, it is an edible salad green. It belongs to the purslane family and is an annual which reseeds itself.

STAKE 2

NURSE LOG. To the right of the trail lies a fallen log. Nurse logs and decaying stumps often form nature's planters for nursling hemlock trees. Sometimes the remnant of a nurse log can still be found at the base of an adult hemlock. (Hemlock is described at Stake 5.) Several mosses occur on or near the nurse log. Most mosses do not have common names.

The MOSS, *Plagiothecium undalatum* has wavy leaves of a light whitish-green color. It clings to rotting logs.

The MOSS, *Eurthynchium oreganum* is a fern-like and feathery moss which grows on logs and rocks. Its stalk is rough to the touch.

SWORD FERN, *Polystichum munitum*, is the most common evergreen fern in this area. Its fronds may reach seventy to eighty centimeters in length. The many leaflets along the stem are triangular blades with a sword hilt where each leaflet attaches. The undersides of the leaflets may have brown spots which contain the spores. The fronds grown in large circular clusters. Sword fern prefers a shaded area. It is a commercially important green in the florist industry.

DOG LICHEN, *Peltigera canina,* is a gray or brownish flat lichen that fans out along the ground. The underside of the lichen is white with root-like rhizoids growing downward. The white underside shows itself as a fringe curling upward.

112

RATTLESNAKE PLANTAIN ORCHID, *Goodyera oblongifolia*, produces a stalk of small, greenish-white orchids. The ground-hugging leaves of dark green are patterned with white lines or streaks. Here, it is found in a moss bed.

STAKE 3

WESTERN RED CEDAR, *Thuja plicata,* like the Douglas fir, it is misnamed and is not a true cedar. True cedars come from the Mediterranean and Himalayan areas. Western red cedar prefers moist sites. Old-growth cedars grow to imposing size--up to six meters (20 feet) in diameter and sixty meters (200 feet) tall. The bark has a reddish cast and is vertically ridged and fibrous. Its leaves are dark yellowish-green scales on flat, frond-like branches. It forms one and a half centimeter cones that stand in upright clusters till the seeds are released. The tree is used to make shingles, shakes, posts, and much lumber. Native Americans manufactured many necessities from cedar, including house planks, canoes, totem poles, clothing, rope, baskets, and mats.

SWORD FERN (description at Stake 2)

SWEET CICELY, *Osmorhiza chilensis*, is a member of the parsley family and resembles Italian parsley with its lower leaves cut into three lobes. Each lobe divides again into three. Upper leaves become smaller, and a stem rising above the leaves bears clusters of tiny white flowers. Both the stem and the leaves are fuzzy.

BRACKEN FERN *Pteridium aquilinum,* is a fern which dies back in winter. It is a paler green than the sword fern and it turns a golden bronze in the fall. Its fronds are triangular. They branch from a main stem to a smaller branch, then branch again. In spring, new shoots, called fiddleheads, curl to form new fronds.

These are edible but are now considered carcinogenic. Bracken also can poison livestock.

HEMLOCK on the right. (Description at Stake 5)

Also notice the dead tree with many woodpecker holes.

SHAGGY MOSS, *Rhyidiadelphus loreus,* is most commonly found on logs and in humus. It has reddish stems with shiny yellowish leaves. The leaves tend to arch and curve backwards.

OCEAN SPRAY on the left. (Description at Stake 5)

OSTRICH-FEATHER MOSS, *Hylocomium splendens*, is an easy moss to identify. It flourishes on soil, decaying logs and soil-covered rocks and can cover a large area. Its reddish stems are scaly and its branches resemble small ferns.

RED HUCKLEBERRY, *Vaccinium parvifolium*, is a deciduous brush. It contrasts with the evergreen huckleberry in that it has red and not blue-black berries. It often grows on stumps or logs in moist conifer forests. Leaves are bright green oval on twigs of green. Its small pink flowers grown singly along the stems.

SITKA or SILKY WILLOW, *Salix sitchensis*, will grow to tree size, thirty-five feet or more. Its green leaves are silvery and hairy on the underside and are wildest above the midsection.

STAKE 4

OREGON GRAPE, *Berberis nervosa*, is one of two Oregon grapes prominent in this area. (The other species, *berberis aquifolium* was described at the start of the nature trail.) The leaflets of this species are more numerous and each stalk carries fifteen to nineteen leaflets. The leaves are less shiny and are flatter and less like holly leaves. Yellow flowers that rise from the crown are less showy than the other species.

CALYPSO ORCHID or FAIRY SLIPPER, *Calypso bulbosa*, is one of spring's delights. The lovely orchid-pink calypso, with its lower or slipper petal of creamy white, tinted with red and yellow dots, grows in rich decaying forest humus. A single dark green leaf clings to the ground, and a slender stem four to eight centimeters tall bears a single flower. Enjoy their light fragrance and delicate beauty, but never pick them.

BEDSTRAW, *Galium aparine*, trails tender square-stemmed vines along the ground and over other plants. It can form a dense, smothering cover. Its leaves grow in whorls, and its small flowers are white. Bedstraw has tiny hooks on stems, leaves and seeds that make it cling to clothing and animal fir--an aid to transporting the seeds.

GRAND FIR, *Abies grandis*, in this area mingles with Douglas fir where sufficient moisture exists. Grand fir is a true fir and is the only true fir growing below 1,500 feet of altitude. It also occurs in higher elevations, up to 5,000 feet. It will grow to 170 feet high. Stiff, straight branches grow from the main trunk. Cones stand upright ten centimeters long and resemble small oval owls. The cones are seldom seen after maturity, since they shed the scales and seeds, leaving only an upright stalk standing like a slender candle. Grand fir buds are yellow-brown and resinous. Its needles--one of the best means of identification--are arranged in two flat rows on either side of a branch. Short and long needles intermingle. They are dark green on top, and are edged with two white lines on the undersides. The needles lie so flat that they look as though they had been ironed. Grand fir is an important producer of lumber and pulp, and it makes an attractive Christmas tree.

HEART-LEAVED TWAYBLADE ORCHID, *Listera cordata*, has two opposite, heart-shaped leaves half-way up its stem.

Small flowers, typically orchid-shaped, at the top of the stem are purple- magenta in color.

SOAPBERRY or BUFFALO BERRY, *Shepherdia canadensis*, may become a fairly tall bush with bright green, oblong leaves with a scaly, brown underside. The brown bark is also scaly and rough. It is an easy bush to identify. Its shiny, bright red berries are very bitter, but were sought by Native Americans who whipped them into a food similar to ice cream.

WOODLAND STRAWBERRY, *Fragaria vesca*, is a member of the rose family. Although it prefers a moist wooded environment, it will grow in open spaces that are not too hot and dry in the summer. Its green leaves and flowers resemble domestic strawberries. Flowers of white to pink make way for tiny red berries which are delicious, but time-consuming to gather.

STAKE 5

Observe the hemlock and grand fir on the right.

WESTERN HEMLOCK, *Tsuga heterophylla*, is designated Washington's state tree. Hemlock trees usually grown in company with western red cedar. Hemlock seeks a moist environment and thrives in shade. Seedlings will grow in the shade underneath other trees. The leader or tip of the tree gracefully curves over instead of standing erect. Small, two centimeters, cones of light brown hang down from the branches. The dark brown bark is fairly smooth, dividing into flat surfaces and fissures. The needles are shorter than those of either douglas fir or grand fir. Once ignored by loggers, western hemlock now is highly valued for lumber.

OCEAN SPRAY, *Holodiscus discolor*, is a deciduous shrub with several trunks grouped together. Its deeply toothed soft green leaves are ovoid in shape. In spring, it ornaments open, brushy areas of the woods with graceful, branching clusters of creamy- white blossoms. The bark is smooth, the wood is tough.

SALAL, *Gaultheria shallon,* carpets much of the floor of our wooded areas. It is a broad-leaved evergreen with large, oval, stiff green leaves. These are finely toothed and pointed at the tip. Small, urn-shaped flowers, pink to white, are borne on one side of the stem. Clusters of dusky purple berries follow the flowers. They are edible, but have numerous seeds and are less juicy than some of the other berries. They are a good food source for birds and mammals. The roots were dug by Native Americas as a winter food supply.

BALD-HIP ROSE, *Rosa gymnocarpa,* is small-flowered, native rose. Its stems are covered with small thorns. Leaves, buds and blossoms are all smaller on this variety than on the Nootka rose. The sepals fall away when the bloom withers; thus its name, bald- hip rose.

SANICLE is described at Stake 1.

STAKE 6

RED ALDER, *Alnus rubra,* is most abundant here. It grows rapidly and prospers in areas where conifers have been logged or burned over. Alders may form thickets in damp places. Male catkins, four to five centimeters long, form in winter and release yellow pollen in early springtime. Seed-bearing catkins resemble miniature pine cones but they grow in clusters. Leaves are oval with prominent veins which give them a ridged appearance. They are also toothed. The trunk is pale gray and fairly smooth. Patches of tiny, scale-like lichens find a home on the bark and form lace-doily patterns. Alders are an important source of nitrogen to the soil.

LICHEN, *Usnea subfloridana,* is a branching, grayish lichen called old man's beard because of its long scraggly appearance. It hangs from the branches of deciduous trees.

NETTLE, *Urtica dioica,* are commonly known as stinging nettle. When touched, they leave a stinging sensation on the skin which can last hours or days. They are perennials that die in the winter and come up from underground creeping shoots in the spring. The oval leaves are coarsely tough and are opposite each other on the stem. Small green flower clusters hang down from the stems at leaf junctures. Stems and leaves are covered with fine hairs. Nettle leaves are brewed as tea and are eaten and cooked as greens. The outer fibers of the dried stems make excellent twine.

MOSS, *Hylocomium splendens*, is described at Stake 2.

RED ELDERBERRY, *Sambucus racemosa,* has clusters of cream-colored flowerlets on upright stalks in the spring, followed in late summer by clusters of bright red berries, each about five millimeters in diameter. The shrub may reach five to six feet in height. Its foliage consists of five to seven long narrow leaflets on each stem.

SNOWBERRY, *Symphoricarpos albus,* is a deciduous shrub found along roadsides and in the woods. It can reach two millimeters in height. It has small leaves and branches an a light airy appearance. Its oval leaves are paired. Pink, tube-shaped flowers are replaced in the summer by tight bunches of white berries which are likely to cling to the bush throughout the winter, adding interest to the landscape.

TRAIL PLANT or PATHFINDER, *Adenocaulon bicolor*, is so named because the fuzzy white underside of the plant's leaves are said to be good trail markers. The leaves are green on top and triangular in shape, slightly indented and toothed. Stems, rising above the plant, bear rather inconspicuous white flowers.

STARFLOWER, *Trientalis latifolia*, sometimes called the Indian potato because of its small potato-like bulbs, is a member of the primrose family. It has little resemblance to primroses, however. A cluster of oval leaves tops the ten to fifteen centimeter plant and mingles with white to pink star-shaped flowers that grow on thread-thin stems.

THIMBLEBERRY, *Rubis parviflorus,* is a busy shrub two to three meters tall. It has light-green, velvet-soft leaves that look much like maple leaves. White, five-petaled flowers, 2.5 centimeters across, precede bright red berries which, like raspberries, pull free from their cores. The tart berries are edible.

LADY FERN, *Athyrium filix-femina*, is a deciduous fern, light green in color. It is most easily identified by the shape of its fronds and by its lack of branching of the main stem. (Bracken fern branches three times from a main stem.) The lady fern frond is widest at its midsection and tapers toward its tip and base. It likes moist soil.

FRINGECUP, *Tellima graniflora*, has toothed, heart-shaped leaves with several lobes, 5-7 centimeters in size. Its hairy stems are as tall as 50 centimeters and carry a string of cup-shaped flowers. Five fringed petals decorate the rim of the flower cup. These flowers turn from greenish-white to rose.

STAKE 7

DOUGLAS MAPLE, *Acer glabrum var. douglasii,* and the big-leaf maple are the two native maples found in the San Juans. The greater size of the big-leaf and its huge leaves make the two species easily distinguishable. The Douglas maple is a deciduous tree which may reach forty feet in height. It is sometimes found in clumps, but each tree has an individual trunk. It likes moist, well-drained areas. Its leaves, 6 to 10 centimeters long, have three to five lobes which are coarsely toothed. Spring brings small, loose clusters of yellowish flowers. Winged, reddish- brown seeds propagate the tree. Pale-yellow fall foliage enhances the landscape. The leaf shape is the one we commonly associate with the Canadian flag and coins.

AT THE INTERSECTION TURN RIGHT

STAKE 8

MOSS, *Leucolepis menziesii,* is an easy moss to identify because its stems stand upright like miniature trees. It reminds one of a forest of tiny firs. This moss favors wet areas and grows on the ground or on decaying logs.

SPOTTED CORAL-ROOT ORCHID, *Corallorhiza maculata,* bears tiny red- brown speckled orchids on a red-brown stem which looks like a red asparagus. The flowers circle the stem near the top of the plant. The plant is leafless and lacks chlorophyll, so it depends on proper soil organisms to nurture it.

Also seen here are SANICLE, SWORD FERN, HEMLOCK, and FIRS.

STAKE 9

LICORICE FERN, *Polypofium yulgare,* is an evergreen fern that grows in mosses and on tree trunks, rocks and fallen logs. It prefers shade and moisture. The leaflets alternate on the stem to form an almost zig-zag pattern. The rhizome has a slight licorice flavor.

INDIAN PIPE, *Monotropa uniflora*, grows in thick rich humus underlying dense woods that allow little light to penetrate to the forest floor. Pale white stems spring up in groups, each bearing a single flower of the same white color. The stem and flower together look like a long slender kaolin clay pope. In winter, only black or brown dried stems and seed pods remain.

STAKE 10

DOUGLAS FIR, described at Stake 1, grows in a grove on the left. It is the primary tree here, but it will eventually be replace by the climax trees, cedar and hemlock, which require less light for propagation and growth.

STAKE 11

ORANGE HONEYSUCKLE, *Lonicera ciliosa*, is a deciduous, tough- stemmed vine that climbs over brush and circles its way up tree trunks as it searches for sunlight.

THE NATURE TRAIL TURNS TO THE RIGHT (UP THE HILL). This is the steepest part of the trail. If this part of the trail is too steep, you may return directly to the parking lot.

As you go up the hill, the trail leaves the shaded forest and leads to an open meadow, cleared years ago for the farm. The large firs at the edge of the meadow have been shaped by the prevailing winds from the Straits of Juan de Fuca.

STAKE 12

MOSS, *Dicranum scoparium*, forms a thick luxuriant carpet-like, green plush. It has yellow-green shoots, slender leaves and reddish stems. It grows in shady spots at the base of trees and on rocks.

CANADA THISTLE, *Cirsium arvense*, plagues the gardener and farmer with its perennial root system which sends up new shoots each spring and with its capacity to spread winged seeds widely. It is a tall plant, 1.5 m, with lavender, fragrant blooms on flower heads, 1.5 cm across. The leaves are coarsely toothed with spines at the edges but not on the tops. The undersides of the leaves bristle with hairs. Canada thistle is an Old World introduction. Goldfinches are attracted to it.

BULL THISTLE, *Cirsium vulgare*, resembles the Canada thistle, but it has larger, deeper-hued, lavender-purple flower heads. It grows to heights of 1 m, so it is not as tall as the Canada thistle. Bull thistle leaves are spiny on top, as well as on the edges. It is a biennial.

CAMAS, *Camassia quamash*, a member of the lily family, is one of spring's beautiful, showy blue flowers. They appear on stems 30 cm tall. The leaves are folded grass-like blades. Camas grows from a small bulb which was an important food item for Native Americans.

PEARLY EVERLASTING, *Anaphalis margaritacea*, sends up gray-green leaves in spring from underground rhizomes. The narrow, pointed leaves are covered with fine white hairs. By late summer, clusters of white flowers with yellow centers form on thick stalks. It can be dried for winter flower arrangements.

THE TRAIL TURNS RIGHT IN THE MEADOW.

Watch for several rolls of rusty barbed wire on the right side of the trail. Most of the area encompassed by this trail was once a farm operated by Mr. & Mrs. John George Jakle. The house and farm buildings stood in the clearing between the barbed wire and the trees. The National Park Service removed the buildings and filled the cellar holes. No evidence of the home or farm buildings remains. Mrs. Jakle's daffodils blossomed for several years after the buildings were removed, but they have disappeared now.

STAKE 13

HAIRCAP MOSS, *Polytrichum juniperinum,* one of our most common mosses, grows even in poor soils. It can survive in dry areas or in very moist areas. Haircap has bluish-green leaves with reddish stalks. Thin stems are topped with a pointed fairy cap which covers the capsules containing spores. The cap has long hairs; thus the common name, haircap.

MOSS, *Rhacomitrium canescens*, covers rocks and rocky knolls with a soft chartreuse carpet. When it dries out, the leaves fold together and have a gray appearance because of their long white tips.

The large boulders in the meadow are glacial erratics deposited more than 10,000 years ago. Many have been transported great distances, so have compositions different from stones native to the area. Gray, black, orange, and yellow lichens grow on the boulders. The view is further enhanced by a dead snag which makes a good perch for eagles and hawks, and by a fallen, weathered, silver-gray log laying at the edge of the firs. This is an excellent place to watch eagles and hawks soaring in the prevailing wind.

TOUR SEVEN: SIGHTSEEING AFTER DARK

The Sen. Jackson viewpoints at American Camp have a special charm after dark. On a clear night, the lights of Victoria are visible on the right and the lights of Seattle are a dim glow on the left. Between them, from left to right, are the lights of Port Townsend, Dungeness, and Port Angeles. The lights of homes on the Olympic Peninsula can also be seen. The major lighthouses are easy to see and identify. A few of the lights are so powerful they are visible on overcast days. The best place to see the lights is the east (second) Sen. Jackson viewpoint at American Camp. The following information is based on that location.

The nearby rotating light on the left is the Cattle Point Lighthouse on San Juan Island. A little to the right of the Cattle Point Lighthouse is a flashing red light on Iceberg Point, on the south end of Lopez Island. To the right of the Iceberg Point light is a cluster of red and white marker lights at Whidbey Island Naval Air Station. These lights do not flash, but in certain atmospheric conditions they seem to twinkle.

To the right of that is a very powerful rotating white light at Point Partridge, on the west side of Whidbey Island. This light is so powerful that it is clearly visible on overcast days.

Looking almost due south is a very powerful flashing red and white light on Point Wilson, north of Port Townsend. The red and white lights appear to flash simultaneously, followed by a long period of darkness.

To the right of the Point Wilson light is a white and green, rotating airport beacon near Diamond Point. This is an "on demand" light. Pilots can activate the light with a radio transmis-

124

sion; it turns itself off a few minutes later. The beacon is very conspicuous when it is on, but it is usually off.

Close to the shore is a flashing green light on a buoy anchored at the end of Salmon Bank. This light is 1.75 miles south of the viewpoint and appears much lower than the other lights.

To the right of the Salmon Bank light, and higher on the horizon, is a flashing white light on the Dungeness Spit, in front of the town of Dungeness.

The large city to the right of Dungeness is Port Angeles. A white and green flashing light can be seen on Ediz Hook, in front of the city. The airport behind the city has a rotating green and white light which is operated "on demand" by pilots.

The rotating green and white airport beacons at the Lopez Island and Friday Harbor airports also are visible from the east Sen Jackson viewpoint. These are "on demand" lights and are infrequently used.

The lights of Victoria glow on the right. Two major navigation lights can sometimes be seen near Victoria. The flashing green light to the left of Victoria is at Trial Island, off the southern tip of Victoria. Another flashing light is on Discovery Island in front of Victoria. It is easier to see these lights from South Beach.

The lights of ships moving through the straits are equally interesting. Ferries and cruise ships are easy to spot because they are bathed in white lights. Freighters, tankers, tugs, and fishing boats display few lights, but they are visible to the careful observer. A ship's direction of travel can be determined from the color of its navigation lights. All vessels display a white light on the mast, a red light on the left (port) side, and a green light on the right (starboard) side. If the red and the green lights are both visible, the ship is moving toward you. When the red light is visible, the ship is moving to your left; when the green light is visible, the ship is moving to your right. If only white lights are visible, the ship may be anchored, but it is probably moving away from you.

Certain ships are required to display special identification lights to assure the safety of nearby ships. The lights most frequently seen in this area are listed below:

Three white lights arranged vertically on the mast--a tug pulling a load 600 ft. long, or longer.

Two white lights arranged vertically on the mast--a tug pushing or pulling a load less than 600 ft. long.

Tugs also display an orange light on the stern.

A green light above a white light on the mast--a trawler or dragger engaged in fishing. This is rarely seen.

A red light above a white light on the mast--usually a gillnetter engaged in fishing. Purse seiners display these lights, but they are restricted to daytime fishing. Gillneters and purse seiners have powerful lights over the work area which are illuminated while the net is set or retrieved.

Index

C

D

E

F

G

H

I

J

K

N

O

P

Q

R

S

T

U

V

W

Z

NOTES

NOTES

BOOKS ABOUT THE COPYRIGHT LAW

William S. Strong, *The Copyright Book: A Practical Guide*, 1984, $16.95.

This book explains copyright protection for books, video, learning modules, computer prorams, art works, etc. It is a valuable guide to creative people who should protect their rights in the works they labor to produce.

Law Books in Review commented: "By and large, the author appears to have succeeded in explaining the law so that a non-lawyer can understand it."

Esther R. Sinofsky, *A Copyright Primer for Educational and Industrial Media Producers*, 1988, 29.95.

"Media producers asked for a book written in plain language that explains the copyright law as it applies to small- and medium-sized production studios. This book identifies manh innocent-looking, but significant legal pitfalls. This book should pay for itself many times over."

To order, send a check or money order for the price of the book, plus $2. for shipping and handling, to:

UMBRELLA BOOKS

PO Box 1460-E

Friday Harbor, WA 98250

ABOUT THE AUTHOR

Jerome K. Miller is the author of six books, and over twenty-five articles. He first visited San Juan Island in 1967, and moved to the island in 1984. Before moving to the island, he taught at the University of Illinois at Urbana- Champaign. His hobbies include cooking, reading, gardening, and San Juan Island lore.